Arts and Refugees

Arts and Refugees
Multidisciplinary Perspectives

Special Issue Editor
Marco Martiniello

MDPI • Basel • Beijing • Wuhan • Barcelona • Belgrade

Special Issue Editor
Marco Martiniello
FRS-FNRS and Liège University
Belgium

Editorial Office
MDPI
St. Alban-Anlage 66
4052 Basel, Switzerland

This is a reprint of articles from the Special Issue published online in the open access journal *Arts* (ISSN 2076-0752) from 2018 to 2019 (available at: https://www.mdpi.com/journal/arts/special_issues/arts_refugees)

For citation purposes, cite each article independently as indicated on the article page online and as indicated below:

LastName, A.A.; LastName, B.B.; LastName, C.C. Article Title. *Journal Name* **Year**, *Article Number*, Page Range.

ISBN 978-3-03921-405-1 (Pbk)
ISBN 978-3-03921-406-8 (PDF)

© 2019 by the authors. Articles in this book are Open Access and distributed under the Creative Commons Attribution (CC BY) license, which allows users to download, copy and build upon published articles, as long as the author and publisher are properly credited, which ensures maximum dissemination and a wider impact of our publications.

The book as a whole is distributed by MDPI under the terms and conditions of the Creative Commons license CC BY-NC-ND.

Contents

About the Special Issue Editor vii

Preface to "Arts and Refugees" ix

Marco Martiniello
Introduction to the Special Issue "Arts and Refugees: Multidisciplinary Perspectives"
Reprinted from: *Arts* **2019**, *8*, 98, doi:10.3390/arts8030098 . . . . **1**

Ruba Totah and Krystel Khoury
Theater against Borders: 'Miunikh–Damaskus'—A Case Study in Solidarity
Reprinted from: *Arts* **2018**, *7*, 90, doi:10.3390/arts7040090 . . . . **3**

Annalisa Frisina and Stefania Muresu
Ten Years of Participatory Cinema as a Form of Political Solidarity with Refugees in Italy. From ZaLab and Archivio Memorie Migranti to 4CaniperStrada
Reprinted from: *Arts* **2018**, *7*, 101, doi:10.3390/arts7040101 . . . . **17**

Hélène Sechehaye and Marco Martiniello
Refugees for Refugees: Musicians between Confinement and Perspectives
Reprinted from: *Arts* **2019**, *8*, 14, doi:10.3390/arts8010014 . . . . **30**

Shannon Damery and Elsa Mescoli
Harnessing Visibility and Invisibility through Arts Practices: Ethnographic Case Studies with Migrant Performers in Belgium
Reprinted from: *Arts* **2019**, *8*, 49, doi:10.3390/arts8020049 . . . . **46**

Cristina Cusenza
Artists from Syria in the International Artworld: Mediators of a Universal Humanism
Reprinted from: *Arts* **2019**, *8*, 45, doi:10.3390/arts8020045 . . . . **63**

About the Special Issue Editor

Marco Martiniello is Research Director at the Belgian National Fund for Scientific Research (FRS-FNRS). He teaches Sociology of Migration and Ethnicity at the University of Liège (Belgium), where he is Director of the Center for Ethnic and Migration Studies (CEDEM) and Vice-Dean of Research at the Faculty of Social Sciences. He has been Visiting Scholar or Visiting Professor at several different universities, including CUNY, NYU, Cornell, and the University of Geneva.

His publications include *Multiculturalism and the Arts in European Cities* (Routledge, 2014); *An Introduction to Immigrant Incorporation Studies. European Perspectives* (Amsterdam University Press, 2014); and *Villes connectées. Pratiques transnationales, dynamiques identitaires et diversité culturelle* (Presses Universitaires de Liège, 2016)

Preface to "Arts and Refugees"

This book focuses on the relevance of the arts and of artistic practices in the actual integration of refugees into the social fabric—a topic which is relatively neglected both in media and political discourse. In the context of the highly polarized public opinion on migration and refugee issues, migrants and refugees tend to be seen either as a threat against which we have to protect ourselves, or as passive victims in need of our help, sometimes in a paternalistic way. Too rarely do we see migrants and refugees as agents, persons who contribute positively to the development of human society in various ways, including through their artistic practices, despite the hardships they are going through. This book contributes to the much-needed counternarrative of migration and asylum. I would like to dedicate it to the thousands of women, men, and children who lose their lives every day, in trying to reach a safe haven.

Marco Martiniello
Special Issue Editor

Editorial

Introduction to the Special Issue "Arts and Refugees: Multidisciplinary Perspectives"

Marco Martiniello

Centre d'Etudes de l'Ethnicité et des Migrations (CEDEM), Faculty of Social Sciences, Liège University, 4000 Liège (Sart-Tilman), Belgium; M.Martiniello@uliege.be

Received: 24 July 2019; Accepted: 1 August 2019; Published: 5 August 2019

Even though the percentage of migrants and refugees in the world has remained relatively stable over the past few decades, in recent years, public debate on this matter has become increasingly sensitive and politicized. The political discourse has become ever more polarized. On the one hand, especially since 2015 when the crisis in Syria reached its peak, the arrival of refugees in Europe and Germany has been seen as a threat against which European countries should protect themselves. The Hungarian Prime Minister, Viktor Orban, decided, with the approval of the Cabinet, to build a 4-m high barrier on the border with Serbia and Croatia in order to prevent asylum-seekers and immigrants from entering the country. The Italian Minister of the Interior and Deputy Prime Minister, Matteo Salvini, has several times declared that no new refugees or migrants should reach Italian ports by sea. He has regularly criminalized rescue NGO's at sea, referring to them as migrant and refugee smugglers. In his view, their activity is not humanitarian but criminal, and they should be sued for their actions. These examples are not unique among European politicians, and they espouse views similar to those of President Trump in the United States (US), who is attempting to end "illegal" immigration and build a wall at the Mexican border. Clearly, policies in the field of migration and asylum have become more and more restrictive and increasingly disregard the very notion of human rights at the core of Western democracies. On the other hand, some politicians have endorsed a more open approach toward migration and asylum, especially at the local level. In the US and in Europe, many cities have declared themselves sanctuary cities, and this action is supported by a significant portion of their populations. Moreover, the transnational movement *refugees welcome* has spread throughout Europe, expressing solidarity with all those who are forced to leave their home country.

In the media and policy debates on migration and refugees, some issues are relatively underexplored, such as the relevance of the arts and of artistic practices in the actual integration of refugees into the social fabric. What is the role of arts (music, theatre, literature, etc.) in the solidarity movements in favour of refugees in European cities and beyond? What are the trajectories of refugee artists and their strategies for claiming a position in their new societies and artistic scenes? This Special Issue discusses these questions, as well as the manifold connections between arts and refugees. The five papers come from different disciplines (i.e., anthropology, musicology and sociology) and different theoretical perspectives and deal with different artistic disciplines (i.e., theatre, cinema, music, visual arts and painting). They all combine a robust theoretical approach with a qualitative empirical case study in different European countries (i.e., Germany, Italy, Belgium and the United Kingdom) and cities (i.e., Munich, Brussels, Liège and London).

In their paper, Ruba Totah and Krystel Khoury present and discuss a theatre project developed in Munich in 2017, where the City Theatre organised the Open Border Ensemble of Munich in which Syrian German artists created a mobile theatre play aimed at minimizing stereotypes and deconstructing essentialist cultural identity prejudices. They show how artistic strategies and relational dynamics came together to give birth to a sort of 'third space'. They also discuss the challenges and implications of such theatre projects for all the participants and for the solidarity between refugees and non-refugees.

Located in the context of the social polarization on migration and refugee issues mentioned above, the paper by Annalisa Frisina and Stefania Muresu shows how participatory cinema has become a way of expressing political solidarity with refugees in Italy. This has occurred over the past 10 years by challenging the mainstream narrative of migration and asylum through the proactive involvement of asylum-seekers in cinematographic work. In a country led by a populist anti-refugee government, solidarity and participation go hand in hand to change the dominant perception of migration and refugee flows.

The third paper, written by Hélène Sechehaye and Marco Martiniello, deals with a musical project by a non-profit organization, *Muziekpublique*, launched in Brussels, the capital city of Belgium and the European Union. *Muziekpublique* specializes in the promotion of so-called "world music". The *Refugees for Refugees* project features traditional musicians from different countries who have found refuge in Belgium. Through this case study, they examine the complexity of elaborating a project that is based on the common identity of "refugees" while simultaneously valuing their diversity. They also discuss the impact of such participatory projects on the musicians' careers and integration in the host country.

The subsequent paper also deals with Belgium. Through an investigation of migrants' objectives in participating in the arts, Shannon Damery and Elsa Mescoli try to understand the different ways in which artistic practices can be used by migrants. Through the exploration of the initiatives of groups of undocumented migrants and refugees involved in artistic activities in two Belgian cities (Liège and Brussels), the paper concludes that art can operate as an empowering tool for migrants, as it constitutes a space for agency, notwithstanding the specific characteristics of the context. It allows migrants to develop strategies of visibility or invisibility, depending on their motivations and aims. Through case studies, the authors claim that art offers opportunities for migrants to actively participate in the socio-cultural and political environment in the host country and to claim various forms of official and unofficial belonging and local citizenship.

Finally, the paper by Cristina Cusenza deals mainly with Syrian visual artists in London. She shows that they are often caught in a process of essentialization and othering regardless of their artistic choices in the discursive register of universalism. Nevertheless, they often organize their lives around the 'Syrian artist' category. Their agency is somehow limited, and their artistic contribution outside of the refugee experience is not easily recognized in the professional art world.

In conclusion, the five articles composing this Special Issue illustrate the complexity of the refugee situation and open up avenues of discussion concerning the role arts can play for refugees in anti-immigration times. At the same time, they also highlight the contribution refugee artists can offer their new country. Let us hope that more research on these issues will emerge in the future.

Conflicts of Interest: The author declares no conflict of interest.

 © 2019 by the author. Licensee MDPI, Basel, Switzerland. This article is an open access article distributed under the terms and conditions of the Creative Commons Attribution (CC BY) license (http://creativecommons.org/licenses/by/4.0/).

Article

Theater against Borders: 'Miunikh–Damaskus'—A Case Study in Solidarity

Ruba Totah [1],* and Krystel Khoury [2],*

1. Institute of Education, Johannes Gutenberg University Mainz, 55116 Mainz, Germany
2. Laboratoire AcTé, Université Clermont Auvergne, 63000 Clermont-Ferrand, France
* Correspondence: rubatotah88@gmail.com (R.T.); Krystelkhoury83@gmail.com (K.K.)

Received: 28 September 2018; Accepted: 19 November 2018; Published: 27 November 2018

Abstract: In 2017, the City Theater of Munich engaged with a policy of diversity, and decided to include Syrian artists and create the Open Border Ensemble. A German and Syrian refugee and non-refugee cast produced the first performance, "Miunikh–Damaskus: Stories of one city" (May 2018). This mobile play aimed at minimizing stereotypes and deconstructing essentialist cultural identity prejudices. The paper examines how, in this case study, multilayered artistic strategies and relational dynamics came together to implement a 'third space'. It addresses the challenges and implications of such theater endeavors regarding solidarity and the representation of the figure of the artists within the realm of the migration and refugee discourse.

Keywords: third space; solidarity; postmigrant theater; representation; improvisation; translation; refugee crisis; cultural policies; relational dynamics; creative process

1. Introduction

In 2015, the German Federal Government opened its doors to an inflow of refugees after it agreed on a pan-European treaty (Dublin III agreement) aiming for equal acceptance of asylum seekers by the state members of the European Union. A mass movement of people seeking refuge, mainly from war-torn countries such as Syria, Iraq, and Afghanistan, reached Germany. With a clear political discourse emphasizing on sharing a 'welcome culture' (Wilkommenspolitik) and activating a policy of integration[1] (Integrationspolitik), the Federal German Government made evident efforts to respond to ethical duties towards refugees, a fact that triggered, in return, critical philosophical public debates on hostility, hospitality, and their limitations (Funk 2016; Jäckle and König 2017). The massive influx of refugees presented a significant social challenge. One way of answering this challenge was to adopt a policy of cultural participation involving local authorities, cultural institutions, as well as independent artists. Artistic activism urged practices of cultural participation. Thus, cities such as Dresden, Göttingen, Hamburg, Mülheim, Berlin, and Munich implemented diverse and numerous artistic as well as sociocultural projects, whether as associative or institutional initiatives[2]. Those projects aimed at bridging people from different backgrounds and stimulating more interaction through art and cultural practices with the people who just arrived. However, a significant shift in policy-making occurred when in March 2016 some EU countries decided to close their borders. This shift was

---

[1] As stated in the Culture and Media Policy of the German Federal Government 2016: "Our society is being increasingly shaped by migration. Cultural participation is a basic precondition for migrants to be able to understand their new surroundings and to be understood by those around them. That is because cultural participation means social participation. And cultural education can play an important role when it comes to boosting cohesion in a heterogeneous, ethnically diverse society".

[2] See: https://www.nachtkritik.de/index.php?option=com_content&view=article&id=11497:immer-mehr-theater-engagieren-sich-fuer-fluechtlinge&catid=1513:portraet-profil-die-neuen-deutschen&Itemid=85.

accompanied in Germany by the increasing popularity of right-wing political parties that made it to the Bundestag for the first time following the results of the 2017 elections. Those changes were going to have repercussions on the local cultural policy regarding the emergence, support, sustainability, and multiplication of artistic endeavors for or with people moving away from crisis areas and escaping conflict zones, as well as on discourses on solidarity and representation.

This article, in line with recent studies focusing on postmigrant theater (Spencer 2016; Komurcu 2016; Petersen and Schramm 2017; Wilmer 2018), is interested in theater experiences as solidarity endeavors where one surpasses the definition of the 'Other' based on geocultural difference. It investigates theater as a medium for discussing issues beyond migration and the 'Migrant' as the 'Other,' rather focusing on the 'living together' with what this entails as multiple dimensions. Current studies in theater and migration closely examine policies of inclusion in Europe (Sharifi 2016) and performative agency within the realm of refugee cultural and political activism (Bhimji 2015), as well as the variety of strategies, like verbatim and autobiographical documentary theater, for addressing problems of migration and the role of nation-states (Wilmer 2018). This case study wishes to discuss this topic from a socio-anthropological perspective based on a recent theater initiative: The Open Border Ensemble OBE at the Münchner Kammerspiele. It presents a microanalysis of a specific situation that took place during the rehearsing process of the performance "Miunikh–Damaskus: Stories of one City", focusing on the relational dynamics emerging out of this living experience and how it shapes a transcultural reality.

2. Data and Method

The analysis relies on participatory observation (Malinowski 1922; Cassell 2012; Charmaz 2014) as a method to collect first-hand qualitative data material. Indeed, the authors of this article, researchers Ruba Totah and Dr. Krystel Khoury, were also directly implicated in the abovementioned theater process: Khoury was the artistic director of the project and Totah was the translator and dramaturgy contributor to the theater production. Other than the ethnographic notes, penetrating insights, and highly contextual understanding brought by the three months of immersion, the corpus data included relevant printed and online communication material produced for the project. They used an empirical approach embedded in ground theory to examine one institutional artistic theater project The Open Border Ensemble initiated by The Münchner Kammerspiele in 2017, and a key moment from the creative process of its first theater production, *Miunikh–Damaskus: Stories of One City*, as a case study.

3. Diverse Institutional Theater Practices

Amidst the shifting political context in Germany in 2015, the art world, including the theater scene, demonstrated various solidarity statements to respond to policies of integration. These statements went hand in hand with initiatives led by artists and cultural operators from the German independent scene following state policies that encouraged cultural participation for integration. Major theater institutions in Germany, like Gorki Theater in Berlin, Schauspiel Hannover, Theater an der Ruhr in Mülheim, Deutsches Nationaltheater Weimar, and lately The Münchner Kammerspiele, opened their doors for theater projects with mainly Syrian and Syrian–Palestinian artists newly established in Germany—with the exception of Weimar and the AZDAR Theater ensemble from Afghanistan and Bremen, with the lately multinational Ensemble New Bremen[3]. Those theaters were trying to conceive midterm projects that aimed to go beyond usual one-shot productions where Syrian artists are working as 'guest artists'. Therefore, in continuation with the German theater tradition of 'Ensembles',

---

[3] Steptext Company and Bremen Shakespeare Company: A cosmopolitan group of eight performers from Syria, Afghanistan, South Korea, Germany, Colombia, Togo, and Senegal to better reflect the diversity of the city.

they implemented each a different model of theater inclusion depending on their artistic mandates and policies.

Starting in 2016, artists were called to form adjacent groups to those theaters' main ensembles. Maxim Gorki[4] Theater created the *Exil Ensemble*. Following a form of theater refugee artist academy, it provided its members with German language and integration courses as well. Schauspiel Hannover[5] initiated, in 2017, the *Yalla Ensemble* to "bring together, around the theater, people from different nationalities residing in Germany, mainly Hannover." Designed as an inclusive socioartistic project, it wished to give the opportunity to artists from Syria and Iraq to work with local youth from Hannover as regular theater workshops trainers and directors of youth theater plays. The Münchner Kammerspiele[6] founded *The Open Border Ensemble* as an experimental transnational collaborative project to resist borders and artistic isolation by calling artists living in Damascus to join the theater, with the aim to open a space for an exchange of expertise. In Mülheim, the group of artists *Collective Ma'louba* aimed to "establish an Arabic-speaking, international artists' collective (...) and develop various interdisciplinary projects which focus on producing Arab-speaking theater performance." While the theater institutions themselves artistically manage all of the above, this collective presented a more hierarchy-challenging structure, claiming a kind of autonomy from the Theater an der Ruhr[7] who are only hosting and supporting in the administration of the collective. The analysis of how each theater introduces its ensemble on their website shows the specific and diverse motivations lying behind their creation. It also reveals that providing a space for an encounter is a common interest, despite the differences those theaters have in funding, audience development, and outreach strategies[8]. Those initiatives are not without facing some challenges.

If being part of those ensembles undoubtedly enables Syrian artists to recover their professional activity, the limited local or federal support questions their sustainability. Moreover, on an aesthetical level, operating under the social integration scheme with the 'refugee crisis' in the background, they have been producing—with only a few rare exceptions—narratives linked to war, forced exile, and escape experiences whether by, with, or for refugees. If those narratives complied at the beginning with the artists' needs to tell those stories and the German audience to hear them, this approach was soon revoked by many Syrian artists who started seeing in it stigmatization and labeling of the Syrian artist outside Syria as foremost a 'refugee artist'[9]. It carried assumptions and expectations towards their artistic production, conditioning their freedom of expression and creativity. From that perspective, it becomes interesting to take those ensembles as socio-anthropological laboratories to examine how they put at stake the construction of representations of newly arrived Syrians artists in Germany.

4. The Open Border Ensemble: Theater against Borders

Until the late nineties, when more practices started to open up to diversity, the German state theater was exclusive and closed to national interests, while the independent theater was more diverse. One of the main challenges of the German institutional theater has long been in its ability to create diversity within its structures and audiences, and in its accessibility by everyone (Wilmer 2018; Spencer 2016; Sharifi 2016). This challenge was to be explicitly addressed by the Münchner Kammerspiele new direction starting in 2015 with the arrival of Matthias Lilienthal. The theater decided to work since then with nonwestern directors from Lebanon, Iran, Japan, Greece, Mexico, and Argentina, to name a few, along with German directors. It invited those artists as associés

---

[4] See: https://gorki.de/index.php/en/company/exile-ensemble.
[5] See: https://www.schauspielhannover.de/index.php?f=07_seiten&ID_Seite=285.
[6] See: https://www.muenchner-kammerspiele.de/munich-welcome-theatre/open-border-ensemble.
[7] See: http://www.collective-malouba.de.
[8] This is due to the histories of each theater institution, as well as social and political contexts of the regions they are based in.
[9] Interviews conducted with artists: Rania Mliehi (2017), Ayham Agha (2017), Shadi Ali (2017), in the framework of the PhD Research Experiences of Syrian and Palestinian Syrian Artists' with The Notion of Refuge by Ruba Totah.

to produce performances for the theater repertoire. Moreover, a specific team *Kammer4you* was formed to work on audience development, organizing themed campuses for students, workshops for kids and teenagers, and presentations, after talks and symposiums. Opening up to a broader, younger, socially and culturally more diverse audience than before, the theater's artistic direction aimed at increasing audience curiosity with artistic productions that reflected more significantly on Munich's shifting demography and its culturally diverse social fabric.

As an engaged city theater, the new team of the Münchner Kammerspiele, unlike other German theaters, showed its concern towards the issue of refugees—their arrival, conditions, and new life in Munich—and was their first station in Germany. Indeed, soon after Germany's borders opened in September 2015, the theater organized The Open Border Congress within the frame of wider project[10] called "Munich Welcome Theater" in October 2015. This congress gathered artists, scholars, activists, and "people who have come to Germany as refugees themselves or are simply interested in coping with the social challenges of worldwide migration movements". It called for a "society of the world that defends openness and diversity", a clear statement of solidarity. The theater later continued its active involvement with the issue of migration and exile by establishing the Welcome Café[11] in April 2016. This format, away from an aesthetic positioning, leaned for more urgent social intervention. It made accessible one of the theater stages as a cultural place for local inhabitants and newcomers to meet, share, and access practical information and take part in cultural events, first weekly then monthly. The ongoing collective commitment expressed a common need to build up alternative narratives. In December 2016, this culminated in the production of the Open Border Ensemble Festival with Arabic-speaking artists and theater amateurs, featuring lectures, stage plays, films, and concerts providing momentum to the Café initiative. After the first rush and solidarity urgency, the theater decided out of this experience to give another configuration to The Open Border Ensemble project and develop it further by trying to shape it, based foremost on an aesthetic theatrical vision. The year 2017 was thus a preparatory year, leading to its implementation as such.

The asylum seekers' migration flow incited the theaters in Germany to work more towards inclusiveness and diversity and adopt transcultural approaches as a form of solidarity. In their article "Putting Flesh to the Bone: Looking for Solidarity in Diversity, Here and Now", Oosterlynck et al. (2016) observe that migration challenges solidarity resources, opens debates on new understanding of citizenship, and is classically based on interdependence, shared norms and values, struggle, and encounter. Thinking on a global level, the Münchner Kammerspiele questioned solidarity beyond the national scope, yet still in connection to it. Its interrogation revolved around how it can be in solidarity with other theater scenes, such as the Syrian one, how it can extend the solidarity scope and expand its borders while answering the urges of the German context, and which collaborative modality to trigger. The team perspective was embedded in postmigration discourses channeling the idea that the migration phenomena are a norm even though the heterogeneity they bring into society is still not reflected enough on German institutional theater stages. After auditions in Munich and Beirut, the theater invited Syrian performers—who had completed their theater studies at the High Institute of Dramatic Arts from Damascus, in Syria—to become part of The Open Border Ensemble (OBE). They were to take part in two theater productions, one of which was *Miunikh–Damaskus: Stories of One City*, directed by Munich-based German director Jessica Glause. This theater project was conceived for a mobile stage to tour in the open air in the suburbs of Munich, meeting new audiences, often unfamiliar with theater. Along the OBE members, this production included a Syrian–Palestinian guest female performer and a German actress from the Münchner Kammerspiele Ensemble. As such, the creative process became a place for encounter on more than one level, carrying the potential of activating transnational solidarity, shifting its understanding from "the bounded

---

[10] This project is funded by Kulturstiftung des Bundes.
[11] An initiative led by Anne Schulz and the Kammer4you team. https://www.muenchner-kammerspiele.de/en/staging/welcome-cafe.

territory of the nation state to the relationally constituted places where diversity is encountered and negotiated" (Oosterlynck et al. 2016).

5. Miunikh–Damaskus: Stories of One City—A Case Study for Creating a 'Third Space'

As its title denotes, *Miunikh–Damaskus: Stories of One City* is a storytelling theater play attempting to explore the possibilities of building a common space. This space, aiming to rethink forms of presentation and open new possibilities, can be considered as a 'third space', to borrow the expression of postmigrant theater scholars (Jeffers 2014; Joseph and Fink 1999; Sharifi 2016). In order to produce the theater piece, director Glause's creative approach used and combined some autobiographical elements provided by the performers as core material. Being the OBE's first production, it brought up the issue of Representation—what did the performers coming from Syria at that moment want to share as stories? Moreover, how and to what extent would these stories represent them? How do they want to position themselves in front of a mainstream German audience? The artistic team of this theatrical project included a director and her assistant, a dramaturg, a translator, a costume designer and her assistant, a music composer, a set designer, and five performers. Its creative process lasted three months, from February until April 2018.

In the following, we focus on a specific key situation we have observed during the creative process out of which we identify improvisation and translation as operating strategies in triggering relations between the director and the performers. We describe the relational dynamics that arose out of the creative process regarding agency and encounter—communications, behaviors, decisions, and self-disclosures. By agency, we refer here to the capability and ability of the performers to act for themselves, as well as about others, while having motivations and resources for the act (Kabeer 1999). We then analyze to what extent the relational dynamics contribute to transforming the theater lived experience into a transcultural reality, the third space.

5.1. Description of a Key Situation: A Rehearsal Session

The following situation took place a week after the beginning of the creative process, on the eighth day during an evening rehearsal. Usually, the team rehearsed in the morning and then in the evening on a four-hour slot. Afternoons were free so that the OBE actors could attend German language classes. The schedule was set on a daily basis, depending on the content of the rehearsal the director decided. Therefore, if most of the rehearsals were collective, some requested the presence of only two or three performers. The situation describes two distinctive moments. The first moment—Moment 1—includes the director, the translator, and two performers: M., a German actress and K., a Syrian actor from the OBE. The second moment—Moment 2—includes all five performers K., H., F., S., and M., the translator, and the theater director.

5.1.1. Moment 1

K. is late. While waiting for him to arrive, M. is on the phone outside the studio. K. arrives and goes in to wear the rehearsal outfit. M. is still downstairs on the phone. The director Glause is annoyed by this delay. She goes out and calls her: "We are starting!" The two performers gather. Glause takes out a paper with a 'nice text' written on it. The text (T), originally in Arabic, is a transcribed story K. has provided in a previous rehearsal. It tells about K.'s own perceptive relationship to the city of Damascus, triggered by the request of the director to talk about Damascus. K. takes a moment to recognize his text and to reconnect with the story told. He then comments: "I guess I am not convinced by it, maybe I should work on it again." The director replies that it could be modified later after they decide how it will be translated on stage by the other actors. She emphasizes that the final text will be given back to the actors and they can rework on it again together with the dramaturg in separate meetings[12]. Glause has a version of the text translated into English. She reads it to M. so that she can get familiar with its content.

Then, Glause explains the task to M.: K. will read the text in Arabic and M. has to tell the text in German, finding her translation technique. The translator sitting next to the director outside the stage will translate out loud the text in English to her. The task requires poli-attentivity, since the telling comprises focusing simultaneously on translating the text from English to German and finding ways to express it and make it understood by a non-Arabic speaking viewer. K.'s voice trembles each time he reads the text, a matter that Glause notices. M. shows much hesitation while trying to complete the task. The director regularly interrupts to give directives and comments on the accuracy of the translation and the performativity of the act of translation. At one point, M. pauses. She asks about the language to be used at the end during the performance. She says she feels more comfortable translating directly from Arabic to German without having the English translation. Glause shows that she understands her concern, but points out that the language used during rehearsals is English—understood by all—but agrees that this makes the situation confusing. They repeat without the intervention of the translator, but M. did not write down the English translation, so she struggles in finding her words every time they start over. In the end, Glause breaks in: "You know, two years ago I told a friend that I would like to work internationally, and now it seems uhhh, I'm lost in translation now." The team takes a break.

5.1.2. Moment 2

After the break, the other performers, N., F. and S. arrive. Glause explains the following: The Syrian performers will tell a story concerning themselves and related to Damascus back in 2008[13]. First, Glause asks K. to read his text (T) while others have to tell the story, over again, using their own styles and techniques. They can support, interrupt, retell, or reinterpret the text of K., but only using physical or vocal expression (like singing). K. starts reading his text in Arabic while M. translates it in German based on the English translation provided by the translator outside the stage, like in Moment 1. In parallel, the other three engage themselves in mime, gestures, and movements, expressing what K. is saying without using uttered words. They try out this configuration three times. Each time, the director asks them not to imitate each other nor repeat the technique they have found, but to try to invent their own way of telling the story. N. uses pantomime, S. uses arms and pointed fingers to draw lines in the space, M. mimes with her hands while translating into German what she hears. F. is given a transparent paper and a pen with a projector. Whatever he inscribes will be projected on one side of the stage wall. He starts drawing.

After a sign from the director, N. starts with his story. He tells it in English. He tells how in 2008, he went around in Damascus with his friends following artists who came to visit the city, taking pictures with them. Years later, he showed it to his father, saying: "This is the Damascus that I like not the one now." Then, it is S.'s turn with the story. She tells, in Arabic, how she was preparing for the championship in Gymnastics in 2008. Suddenly, she pauses with tears in her eyes. She continues her story, weeping. Every time one of them starts telling his personal story, the others are asked to create images with their postures or signs of what is being told, while M.'s task with the help of the translator is to translate in German. While narrating, the performers pause for a moment to allow the translation process. They listen to the translations that are taking place in parallel.

It is F.'s turn. He decides to explain his drawing. A moment of tension arouses: His fellows, except M., show disagreement because he did not follow the director's instruction. Instead of using

---

[12] It is after several discussions (collective and individual) and many dialogs between the performers, the director, the dramaturg, the artistic director of the OBE, and translator aiming at working on the style and sharpening the meanings transmitted that the director gave the performers a final manuscript. Some adaptations resulted from discussions during rehearsal breaks. A prolonged period of writing extended the creative process before a final manuscript was ready.

[13] In 2008, Syria saw a prosperous moment in its history after the country started to open to the international market. The same year also marks the year of Damascus Arab Cultural Capital, with a vivid cultural program promoting local and international artistic events. This year was chosen by the director because one of the performers mentioned it in his improvisation.

the transparent paper and the projector to translate the stories, he did an incomprehensible drawing. Following this, M. wishes to know what the drawing was about, so F. explains what it represents: The 'Amawi' (Umayyad) square, a landmark in Damascus, with its sword; and Barada river. However, what is inside the river is not fish. Fish has turned into bombs or eyes of dead people. K., who was supposed to have his story drawn by F., is drowning in the river. Moreover, his feet are held by a rope that is growing bigger and bigger, forming what F. calls 'the idea of Syria', 'a big one'.

5.2. Strategies for Constructing a 'Third Space'

5.2.1. Improvisation

In order to construct the performance, Glause's general creative process approach can be summed up as follows: First, she triggers the memory of the actors and actresses in order to bring out personal stories. She then selects the ones relevant to the storyline of the play by trying to combine, as much as possible, common stories from the daily life of the performers in order to find connections between the different places they come from. She then organizes one-to-one meetings for style assertion and discussion. This dialogical approach introduces a relationship between her and the actors away from a direct hierarchy. The themes tackled are related to the city, memories, dreams, and personal perceptions when changing spaces, and this is maybe what characterizes Miunikh–Damaskus stories compared to what Woolley (2017) identifies as the 'asylum story'. Unlike the depicted process by Woolley of constructing an 'asylum story' that results from a process of revisions practiced in a hierarchy by translators and administrative and legal representatives during hearing sessions, the stories of Miunikh–Damaskus move away from this narrative. They focus on offering new images and experiences of Damascene life that are rarely told by the mainstream media. This choice is also related to the fact that other than one performer who has a refugee status that shaped her relationship to the space, the others had just arrived to Munich to work as actors. The narrative was thus constructed around personal stories from a war zone area—which emphasized the transcultural aspect of this theater process. This environment comprises no legal decision maker in front of the narrator, yet relates the Syrian performers in Germany to the refugee crisis in general by the simple fact of being Syrian citizens. They become, like Cox would write, "authorized non-citizens" in the sense of citizens with temporally limited rights to move to and within nations.

This dialogical approach in constructing the narrative calls for a triangulation (Cox 2018) made by most verbatim[14] theater "narrative, validation and innocence (morality of the human story)" in order to guarantee situating the story within a humanizing paradigm and to enable possibilities for imaginative audience engagement. The dialogical approach in the creative process aims at building up trust to achieve this triangulation and make the actors tell more stories easily during rehearsals. It facilitates sharing the stories that would become a creative resource for the performance. It also empowers the director in her leading role and maintains her authority in the triangulation and the formation of the story. It is only after this connection is made that she delivers back to the performers the material selected and reconfigured by her for dual or collective semidirected improvisation sessions.

The observed situation describes one of the rehearsal sessions characterized by a layering of improvisations. Indeed, it builds upon previous days of improvised material, but also creates new ones. Here, improvisation as a theater practice allows personal stories to emerge and be told for the first time as raw material. It also pushes the performers to find creative techniques to transmit those stories beyond language, including the use of drawing to construct other fictional stories inspired by the original personal story. Each actor discloses a personal story. By asking them to repeat the task, the director orients the performers to recreation and to enhance a new way of transmitting the

---

[14] According to Cox, it is a subset of documentary theater devised wholly or in part from the words of real people and has oral testimony at its heart. Practitioners of the form often regards their work as intervening in the public record, offering new or alternative accounts of events (145).

story of the other. While she does not play the role of the decision maker who seeks the discoverable truth, as Woolley (2017) calls the 'truth finder', she practiced her role to lead the invention of new means of connecting the stories of the performers together. Repeating opens to them the possibility to re-appropriate their story, disrupting the director's authority, and also to identify or at least to familiarize themselves with the stories of their fellows. However, the director's artistic directives, interposing regularly the flow of the improvisation session to keep up with the storyline, assert back her authority position.

In the interviews led with the performers during the project, K. perceives the use of improvisation as a tool to introduce oneself to the other and vice versa by experimenting with unusual methods. He says it encourages the creation of a comfort zone, opening up for self-experimentation and evaluation, surprise, and self-content. Additionally, unlike his previous professional experiences based on written plays, the improvisation session is led in this process by 'a supportive authority' that continually encourages new ways of expression. While F. sees in the improvisation sessions too much authority, it compromises his free space as an actor. However, he adds that those sessions call for activating practices of adaptation to overcome the challenge.

In Moment 1, the uttered sentence of K.: "I guess I am not convinced by it. Maybe I should work on it again," to which the director responds with "later", reveals a cognitive process encompassing the capability to act even if still concealed in the rhetoric. Indeed, the verb 'guess' indicates the awareness of the actor towards a certain reality, 'convinced' indicates a decision making, and 'work' indicates a possible action. It reveals a confrontation with himself. Similarly, for M., although her hesitation, pause, and questioning in the middle of the exercise denote a certain feeling of discomfort, she takes action by stating that she prefers not having the English translation, a matter that would put her in a struggling position afterward when rehearsing. Although the director justifies the process, she accepts the request of M. Later, in an interview, M. explains that within such a multilingual context and diversity in acting styles and cultural backgrounds, she believes using improvisation, in general, is a difficult experience. However, if it makes it more difficult to cope with the transcultural situation, it also challenges her to break out of her comfort zone and start a process of self-experimentation, activating her abilities to contribute to the needed collective aspect of this particular theater-making experience. In Moment 2, F. follows the task of using drawing while drifting from it at the same time: He does not translate his peer's story, but invents a new one which differentiates him from others, yet puts him in an isolated position regarding his peers who show disagreement. Additionally, while K. tells his story, others are encouraged to support or to interrupt by telling their stories. The actors mostly interrupt and, therefore, the stories do not develop collectively. This repeats when M. stands against his peers' disagreement to share the story of F. They extend the confrontation with the self to include a confrontation with the other. It makes the other a constituent of the confronted self.

Other confrontations described in the interviews are related to external factors to this transcultural improvisation experience. K. says that he is not sure if his stories will be interesting for the audience being put on stage that way: Whether the decisions resulting from confrontations and negotiations he engaged in with peers and with the director to develop this performance will be meaningful to audience. Further, M. described that she needed peer-support from German actors in dealing with such a multicultural project. F. described a need to create imaginative spaces about the city of Munich which could have enriched his improvisations and minimized his alienation from the venues, the city, the audience, and the artistic decisions in the project.

Those confrontation moments can be called endurance-in-the-self moments that are expressed, whether before action (case of K.), or accompanied by action (case of M. and F.), or following the action. They are key instants illustrating processes of agency formation, allowing the performers to have the space to develop their self-image and negotiate it, showing their singularities. This deconstructs the attempt for any collective representation of the 'Syrian Artist'. By doing so, actors expose to the director and the group a subjective representation of themselves. They describe situations where the performers are actively engaged in the theater process of negotiating their position within the group. They are triggered by the main theater creative tool used throughout this creative process: Improvisation.

More than a creative tool, improvisation operates as a strategy through which the performers are able to position themselves as agents regarding the directive authority and peers. They can activate their agencies, their capacities as individuals to act independently, by expressing, changing, transposing, transforming, and extending stories and standpoints. Improvisation operates as a strategy to regulate the asymmetrical relational configurations (Simmel 1999) and the confrontations emerging between the performers and the director, which determine or limit their decisions as agents, as well as between the performers themselves as a heterogeneous group with different acting approaches and cultural backgrounds. It encourages what Woolley (2017) describes as the hybrid prose formation of stories which results from enhanced agencies in the processes of sharing their stories. It creates a 'third space', which is not the addition of the performers' spaces and the director's space, nor a binary oppositional representation of each, but another emerging space of ongoing tension and negotiation.

5.2.2. Translation

With a Syrian and German cast, the Miunikh–Damaskus creative process raised the issue of language. The director openly addressed this matter from the start as a challenge to be surpassed. Sentences such as "How do we manage language together?", "How to avoid misunderstandings?", "How to initiate a space to know each other?", "This will be important for our work, especially that there are three languages," "the most difficult thing is the language now," punctuated her introductory speech on the first day of rehearsals. In this transnational project, German, Arabic, and English—as the common working language—were used. Moreover, aware of the essential role translation plays as a precondition to the construction of any shared space and to facilitate the communication process, the theater direction appointed an interpreter. The interpreter fulfilled many functions, from direct translation to transcription to cultural mediation. She translated the conversations between the director and the performers. She also translated the directives of the director to the Syrian performers during the sessions and what they were improvising. To be able to select the parts she was interested in, the director used a recorder. The interpreter was also responsible for providing a written translation of the recorded selections to the director, who would bring those texts again to the working sessions. Those texts formed the written material based on which the performers would create a scene. Thus, translation comprised technically translating the communication around the artistic material that is mainly facilitating the communication between the director and the Syrian performers, as well as translating to English the content of the material improvised by the performers in Arabic.

In Moment 1, Glause brings a text (T) in its English and Arabic version, narrating a personal story of K. that was recorded during a previous improvisation session. She gives as a task to M. to translate it to German while K. is reciting it in Arabic. Similarly, in Moment 2, she asks the other performers to physically translate the story of K. The session revolves around how to best translate K.'s text on stage using creative methods so that, later on, the German audience understands it. By giving this task to the performers, Glause not only put translation at the core of the communication process between the participants, but also literally put the translation process on stage as one of the main subjects of the theater piece itself. Indeed, to ask the actors to translate becomes a typical task in the following improvisation sessions. By adding layers of translation in the scene (Moment 2), the text goes through a continuous process of transformation of the meaning. The performers attempt to transmit, in their own language, the story of their peer told in another language (M.'s case). They improvise new ways of conveying its content (H. and S.'s case). Moreover, depending on the medium used (body, projector), each time they translated, they added a new layer of comprehension to the extent of creating a new story inspired by it (F.'s case). More than a communication tool, translation operates as a creative strategy in paving the way towards a third common space.

Like improvisation, the use of this strategy also shaped the relational dynamics between the director and the performers in a challenging way. The fact of insisting on creating a multilingual theater play where the mother tongues of the participants are different was a way to acknowledge the cultural specificities against assimilation. It empowered their agencies. Although K. could speak English, he systematically chose Arabic in all improvisations. Although M. was not sure of what K. was saying, word-by-word in Arabic, she revoked the translation in English, wanting to improvise/translate directly in German. However, the director's recurrent interruptions were shifting back the power balances to gain her leading position again. A position constantly challenged by the fact of having to write a text with source material in a language she cannot understand (Arabic), translated in another language that is not her mother tongue (English) but that operates as a translanguage in such a plurilinguistic team. It is by making translation central to the creative process and maintaining a specific collectivity through a shared language that the director practiced her authority. She brought legitimacy to the stories within her play storyline by multiplying them with several languages and bringing a reiterated story opposed to what Woolley described as the 'asylum story' by maintaining aspects of 'home narratives'. Her concluding sentence in Moment 1, 'You know, two years ago I told a friend that I would like to work internationally, and now it seems uhhh, I'm lost in translation now,' reveals the ambivalent nature of translation. Translation enabled the construction of a transcultural space and opened up possibilities to unravel indeed, and sometimes to resolve conflicts arising from oral miscommunication and to go beyond differences, yet it reminds of the presence of those differences. This reminder kept the negotiations between actors and the directive authority ongoing.

In Moment 1, M. pauses the translation and steps out, requisitioning the efficiency of this tool within the creative act, especially that as much as this translation was facilitating the creative process, it was interrupting her creative agency as an actress. Learning the stories of her peers through this translation routine took place amidst recurrent interruptions. However, in the performance on stage, she became an agent of those stories. Translation stimulated self-confrontation moments for M., where she had to develop her role from being an actor into creating a new image of herself of becoming an actor–translator. Meanwhile, K. is confused every time he reads the text and listens to its double translation (English and German). Hearing his own story again confronted him with it and with the director's creative process. Similarly to Moment 2, even if the voice of the translator in the rehearsal space tries to adapt emotionally to the improvised situation, it imposes a certain rhythm: The actors have to systematically stop and listen to the translation while improvising and confronting themselves to their own stories.

In addition, In Moment 2, interpersonal confrontations create situations of 'tremble', 'hesitance', 'pausing', and 'struggling', which influence the communication between actors by continually distorting the messages, emotions, and follow-up processes by the other actors while they create scenes. In Moment 1, M. continues to develop her translation skills without reference to the paper, even though she later describes how difficult the improvisation process was to her. Her resilience was confronting her with cultural difference and preparing her for another confrontation with the audience in the final performance. This confrontation included a new representation of herself as an actor–translator of a multicultural third space. Translation operates as a strategy that regenerates difference and stimulates new positions of performers as agents to constantly negotiate this difference. It enables them to activate their agencies as individuals to give meaning to the shared space of cultural difference negotiations, the 'third space'.

The microanalysis of the observed situation and the identification of the multilayered creative strategies in use demonstrate the mechanisms through which a transborder theater experience is built up, constantly shifting between drawing limits and then crossing limitations between the self and the others. Improvisation is about the creation and recreation of stories and situations, whereas translation is about communicating and connecting people and raising challenges, understandings, and ideas. They involve the self and the other. As such, they both function as strategies to transform the creative process into a third space as a relational experience. It is an experience of disorder and confusion where agents have to confront themselves simultaneously and encounter with others, reconsidering their habitual routines. It is within this relational tension that a transcultural reality unfolds. It starts being constructed as soon as the stories, outspoken and traveling across a geographical boundary, are shared, multiplied, and transformed. Throughout this process, the performers are urged to rethink, be more aware of what they present and represent, and contemplate to find motivations to redefine themselves in a new place that is in motion.

6. Discussion

6.1. Third Space and Solidarity

Relational dynamics discussed in the case study correspond to what is seen by Gelfand et al. (2006) as envisioning the self as in its relationship with the other, where negotiation of representation involves both the self and the other. The relational dynamics within this transcultural reality describe practicality on the interventions on the concept of the 'third space', which refer to a medium of new possibilities for translating cultural difference, maintaining plurality, and challenging the authoritative forms of control and challenging binaries (Joseph and Fink 1999; Sharifi 2016). The third space of OBE is constructed within the framework of the German theater institution solidarity with issues of migration and flight. While solidarity motivates establishing adjacent ensemble models, one main challenge to this solidarity approach is that ensembles, like OBE, are subject to conditional funding and limited duration. This conditions the migration phenomena to a limited temporary social determinant and limits the space for broader and larger solidarity. In an interview, Glause says: "I planned to discuss some issues about the project with the theater administration, but then I realized that this experience is happening only once, it's not happening again."(Glause 2018) This temporality of engaged practices challenges the sustainability of the concept of the 'here and now'. Temporality can refer to a 'utopian performative' (Dolan 2002) which creates a temporal space for critique, perspectives, difference, and a practice of the identity of the other through translation and improvisations to negotiate beliefs on the bases of these differences. It stimulates 'a structure of feelings' among actors and actresses as they engage in this temporal space. If solidarity is 'nurtured through the very practices people jointly engage in diverse places' in the here and how (Oosterlynck et al. 2016, p. 12), then temporality becomes essential to the theater as a practice of solidarity. The legal state of authorized noncitizenship and other states of 'unauthorized noncitizenships' (theater makers in exile whose transnational mobility is 'unauthorized') maintains an unsteady ground for joint human-paradigm based practices of solidarity (Cox 2018). The postmigrant theater scholarly efforts in Germany call for beyondness in critically and reflexively discussing migration in theater and the Open Border Ensemble presents its members within the scope of this beyondness. The above microanalysis proposes improvisation and translation as strategies to create a third space of beyondness, where moments of enduring-in-the-self are practiced in larger temporal and artistic scopes, and where solidarity is continuously constructed within theater relational dynamics.

The theater institutions solidarity statements, as well as the mechanisms of establishing the OBE and third space creation strategies, contribute to the Syrian, the artist, and the refugee-artist figures and representations in German society. In the research on solidarity in diversity, solidarities grow as people practice life experiences together in diverse places, relationally. Being citizens of specific legal entities could be overcome by finding innovative forms of solidarity elsewhere that consider the specific situation of the encountered practice and the time span when this encounter happened (Oosterlynck et al. 2016). Then, citizenship is defined by acts and interpersonal practices of diverse individuals, their representations, and their varying positions in the society sphere (Ibid., p. 13). This case study builds on this political and social perspective of solidarity by stressing that within a single encounter practice over a time span reside various representing mediums that are guided by the agency of individuals.

6.2. Third Space Strategies

If improvisation is a strategy for a 'third space' that deals with creating, recreating, and negotiating stories and representations of the Syrian actors of the OBE, improvisation could become a strategy of the overall transnational experience of OBE members in Munich. Cultural participation of Syrian artists in this case study constitutes a nexus of their artistic activism and the disorder/reorder processes of their life routines. In addition to the negotiations they are involved in during the creative process, it includes the simplest personal behaviors that the artists coming to Germany had to reconsider as a consequence of their moving, for example, reorganizing life habits, and moving away from comfort zones: Changing sleep routines, excess sweating while sleep, dropping off phone calls routines and transport habits from and to the workplace. In addition to life habits, they experience an active reorganizing of work conditions and contracting processes, work permits, registration at the city departments, city infrastructural routines, weather conditions, language requirements, and content prepreparation.

Improvisation is explained by Montouri (2003) as the state when a decision is made to deviate from order, where the best thing to do is to improvise, knowing that there will be a return back to order at some point. Creating a third space can be considered the OBE members' negotiation, deviation medium, from a fixed understanding of the self. This medium is temporal, where encounters are extended and deepened to illuminate the cultural difference in the creative process before a new common understanding is derived or before the deviation ends. This extension may be prolonged until moments of evaluations, contemplation of individual representations are given enough space to occur, and where collective agencies are eventually forming to provide new meanings and new representations of cultural differences. This third space turns the deviant approach into a strategy, which opens possibilities for new representations, affiliations, and solidarity.

In addition to improvisation, the translation strategy contributes to the construction of relational dynamics among OBE members. In literature, the translation layers of the OBE fall into several styles but mainly relate to 'community interpreting', which almost all OBE members practiced in certain moments, and mainly resembles the actor–translator role of the German actor. Community interpretation as a practice of volunteers, untrained bilinguals, friends, and relatives is an active, communicative tool that involves face-to-face interaction and emphasizes the role of the translator as both a language and a social mediator (Baker and Saldanha 2009). This form of translation is mostly practiced in this case study by the German actress, who eventually transforms the third space into a community space, a social medium of interaction. As the translation strategy coincided with the improvisation process, it managed to create what Spivak (2009) calls an 'intimate act of reading' that closely attempts to comprehend the stories of participants, to realize the limits of the knowledge to translate them. As a strategy, it continuously uncovers confrontations of the self regarding what it realizes as a lack of knowledge about others. It ceases to be a technical activity, but a 'subject-constituting process' which constantly shuttles between interior and exterior, between self and other, between individual and collective (Bala 2014). Translation in Miunikh–Damaskus shuttles between the interior and the exterior, in the self and the other of its members, enabling a better understanding of emerging representations of artists. Doing so over a period of time, solidarity space aided by this medium of translation is no longer in finding common space between artists, but in the experiencing and learning of each other within a third space. Solidarity in the Miunikh–Damscus theatrical experience is thus stretched beyond common grounds to interpersonal practice over an extended period of time.

Author Contributions: For this article, conceptualization, methodology, writing—original draft preparation, writing—review and editing, investigation for Sections 3 and 4 are the work of both authors R.T. and K.K. Investigation for Sections 5 and 6, data validation, resources are the work of R.T. All other statements are not applicable.

Funding: This research received no external funding.

Acknowledgments: The authors would like to acknowledge for their support Professor Cornelia Schweppe-Johannes Gutenburg University Mainz, Mophradat Art Fellow Program 2017–2018, DAAD, The Münchner Kammerspiele, Kammer4You, Miunikh-Damascus team and The Open Border Ensemble performers.

Conflicts of Interest: The authors declare no conflict of interest.

References

Agha, Ayham. 2017. Interview by Ruba Totah. Theatre Director and Actor, Maxim Gorki Theatre. Personal interview, Berlin, Germany, May 5.

Ali, Shadi. 2017. Interview by Ruba Totah. Freelance Actor and Singer. Personal interview, Munich, Germany, July 3.

Baker, Mona, and Gabriela Saldanha. 2009. *Routledge Encyclopedia of Translation Studies*. London: Routledge.

Bala, Sruti. 2014. 'Translation Is the Making of a Subject in Reparation': Elfriede Jelineks Response to Fukushima in Kein Licht. *Austrian Studies* 22: 183–98. [CrossRef]

Bhimji, Fazila. 2015. Collaborations and Performative Agency in Refugee Theatre in Germany. *Journal of Immigrant and Refugee Studies* 1: 1–23. ISSN 15562948It.

Cassell, Catherine. 2012. Participant Observation. In *Essential Guide to Qualitative Methods in Organizational Research*. London: SAGE.

Charmaz, Kathy. 2014. *Constructing Grounded Theory*. Los Angeles: SAGE.

Cox, Emma. 2018. Postcolonial Noncitizenship in Australian Theatre and Performance: Twenty-first-Century Paradigms. In *The Bloomsbury Introduction to Postcolonial Writing: New Contexts, New Narratives, New Debates*. London: Bloomsbury Academic, pp. 141–57. ISBN 9781474240079.

Dolan, Jill. 2002. Finding Our Feet in the Shoes of (One An) Other: Multiple Character Solo Performers and Utopian Performatives. *Modern Drama* 45: 495–518. [CrossRef]

Funk, Nanette. 2016. A spectre in Germany: Refugees, a 'welcome culture' and an 'integration politics'. *Journal of Global Ethics* 12: 289–99. [CrossRef]

Gelfand, Michele J., Virginia Smith Major, Jana L. Raver, Lisa H. Nishii, and Karen O'Brien. 2006. Negotiating Relationally: The Dynamics of the Relational Self in Negotiations. *Academy of Management Review* 31: 427–51. [CrossRef]

Glause, Jessica. 2018. Interview by Ruba Totah. Theatre Director. *Personal interview*, Munich, Germany, May 9.

Jäckle, Sebastian, and Pascal D. König. 2017. The dark side of the German 'welcome culture': Investigating the causes behind attacks on refugees in 2015. *West European Politics* 40: 223–51. [CrossRef]

Jeffers, Alison. 2014. *Refugees, Theatre and Crisis: Performing Global Identities*. London: Palgrave Macmillan.

Joseph, May, and Jennifer Fink. 1999. *Performing Hybridity*. Minneapolis: University of Minnesota Press.

Kabeer, Naila. 1999. Resources, Agency, Achievements: Reflections on the Measurement of Women Empowerment. *Development and Change* 30: 435–64. [CrossRef]

Komurcu, Onur. 2016. Post Migrant Theatre and Cultural Diversity in the Arts: Race, Precarity and Artistic Labour in Berlin. Ph.D. Dissertation, University of London, Goldsmiths, UK.

Malinowski, Bronislaw. 1922. Argonauts of the Western Pacific, 1st ed. London: Routledge & K. Paul, New York: Dutton E.P.

Mliehi, Rania. 2017. Interview by Ruba Totah. Dramaturg, Schauspieler, Hannover. *Personal interview*, Hannover, Germany, April 28.

Montouri, Alfonso. 2003. The complexity of improvisation and the improvisation of complexity: Social science, art and creativity. *Human Relations* 56: 237–55. [CrossRef]

Oosterlynck, Stijn, Maarten Loopmans, Nick Schuermans, Joke Vandenabeele, and Sami Zemni. 2016. Putting Flesh to the Bone: Looking for Solidarity in Diversity, Here and Now. *Ethnic and Racial Studies* 39: 764–82. [CrossRef]

Petersen, Anne Ring, and Moritz Schramm. 2017. (Post-)Migration in the Age of Globalisation: New Challenges to Imagination and Representation. *Journal of Aesthetics & Culture* 9: 1–12. [CrossRef]

Sharifi, Azadeh. 2016. Theater and Migration. In *Independent Theatre in Contemporary Europe: Structures—Aesthetics—Cultural Policy*. Bielefeld: Transcript.

Simmel, Georges, ed. 1999. Domination et subordination. In *Sociologie. Etudes sur les formes de la socialization*. Paris: PUF, pp. 161–265. First published 1908.

Spencer, Stephen. 2016. *Race and Ethnicity: Culture, Identity and Representation*. Abingdon: Routledge.
Spivak, Gayatri Chakravorty. 2009. *Outside in the Teaching Machine*. New York: Routledge.
Wilmer, Stephen E. 2018. *Performing Statelessness in Europe*. Cham: Palgrave Macmillan.
Woolley, Agnes. 2017. Narrating the Asylum Story: Between Literary and Legal Storytelling. *Interventions* 19: 376–94. [CrossRef]

© 2018 by the authors. Licensee MDPI, Basel, Switzerland. This article is an open access article distributed under the terms and conditions of the Creative Commons Attribution (CC BY) license (http://creativecommons.org/licenses/by/4.0/).

Article

Ten Years of Participatory Cinema as a Form of Political Solidarity with Refugees in Italy. From ZaLab and Archivio Memorie Migranti to 4CaniperStrada

Annalisa Frisina [1],* and Stefania Muresu [2],*

[1] Department of Philosophy, Sociology, Education and Applied Psychology, University of Padua, Via Cesarotti 10/12, 35123 Padova, Italy
[2] Independent sociologist and film-maker, Association 4CaniperStrada, 07100 Sassari, Italy
* Correspondence: annalisa.frisina@gmail.com (A.F.); stemuresu@gmail.com (S.M.)

Received: 12 October 2018; Accepted: 3 December 2018; Published: 6 December 2018

Abstract: This paper introduces the context of European mobilizations for and against refugees and how participatory cinema has become a way of expressing political solidarity with refugees in Italy. We present and discuss ten years of the artistic work of ZaLab and Archivio Memorie Migranti and focus on two film projects of 4CaniperStrada. Central to the production of participatory cinema in Italy is challenging the mainstream narrative of migration through the proactive involvement of asylum seekers, with their political subjectivity, by using a self-narrative method.

Keywords: documentary films; participatory video; refugees; political solidarity; Italy

1. Introduction

As Della Porta underlines in her book on European mobilizations for and against refugees' rights (2018), in the last decade securitization of migration has led to a reduction in the legal channels of migration and a proliferation of legislation to limit and hierarchize citizenship, with the criminalization of undesirable migrants and the normalization of detention and deportation as instruments of governance. Repression has expanded from the targeting of migrants to the legal persecution of activists from grassroots groups and NGOs. Radical right-wing groups have worked as entrepreneurs of fear and hate against "others".

In Italy, which is at the frontline of the long "refugee crisis", solidarity activists have enacted a variety of direct social actions (i.e., emergency provision of food and clothes; help with communication; managing of informal refugee camps; hosting of migrants within and outside the governmental reception system[1]) and different forms of protest (local protests to denounce the conditions of migrants and demand changes in the reception system; symbolic actions at the border with other European countries to denounce the obstacles to the freedom of movement of asylum seekers; opinion campaigns to demand changes in the management of the governmental reception system; solidarity marches as a response to anti-migrant actions). Activists have shown a pragmatic attitude and different levels of contentiousness (Zamponi 2018). They have converged on the idea of solidarity, though the

---

[1] The reception of refugees and asylum seekers in Italy is handled by three different systems: CARA (Centres of Reception for Asylum Seekers), CAS (Centres of Extraordinary Reception), and SPRAR (System of Protection for Asylum Seekers and Refugees), which answer to the Ministry of the Interior. The local representatives of the Ministry of the Interior, the prefects, are in charge of the structures and camps in which asylum seekers are hosted. These structures are often owned by NGOs or private citizens, who receive government funds (Zamponi 2018, p. 103).

understanding of the concept varies according to different groups and with the passing of time (Della Porta 2018, pp. 340–42): from compassionate help to the right to hospitality; from the right to move to the right to stay in dignified conditions.

A tension has emerged between the "humanitarian narrative"[2] (considering refugees as victims) and a more political vision of solidarity (recognizing migrants' agency, establishing more symmetrical relationships, searching for partnerships and coalitions).

Social movement scholars have paid attention to the *framing* process (what issues are at stake?)[3] and the need to convince different players (insiders and outsiders), also through the mobilization of emotions. In the last decade, a growing number of social documentaries have challenged dominant frames on contemporary migrations in Europe[4]. To quote Vittorio Iervese (sociologist and current director of the Festival dei Popoli, International Documentary Film Festival-based in Florence), "brave and uncomfortable documentary" has challenged what mass (and social) media do not show about migrants and refugees in Italy[5]: above all the agency and the active participation of migrants in their representations (Iervese 2016, p. 133).

Migrant cinema[6] has played an important cultural role in the conflictual transformations of European society[7] and today it looks at wider socio-political processes related to colonial legacies and new forms of colonialism by showing how those who have been kept invisible continue challenging material and symbolic borders (Ponzanesi 2011). Migrant cinema has become a form of activism, i.e., fighting racism against migrants. Suffice to think of the pioneering experience of the migrant-cineaste Alvaro Bizzarri, who emigrated from Italy to Switzerland in the seventies (La Barba 2018). Like other citizens of foreign origin, Bizzarri suffered widespread racism and it was his indignation at the expulsion of the children[8] of seasonal workers which turned him to film. His cinematographic accounts aimed to make migrants take consciousness of their condition[9] and to trigger self-organization and solidarity (above all class solidarity). Bizzarri's cinematographic gaze took an antiracist stance, it was a rejection of the then-dominant imaginary which dehumanized Italian workers in Switzerland and

---

[2] For a critique of humanitarianism, see (Fassin 2010).

[3] The concept of framing derives from Erving Goffman's *Frame Analysis* (1974) and it is widely used in all social sciences (for an introduction in the field of communication, Barisione 2009). Applied to social . . . movements (Snow 2004), the idea of *framing* suggests that meanings are constructed through interpretative processes and they are contestable. Social movement leaders and participants (as well as their opponents) regularly engage in this conflictive signifying work.

[4] See for example the works of Fernand Melgar (http://www.swissfilms.ch/de/film_search/filmdetails/-/id_person/3059), in particular "Vol special" (free available at https://vimeo.com/111191661, last accessed on 9 October 2018), distributed in Italy by ZaLab.

[5] Vittorio Iervese was the curator of two cycles of films selected "to rebel against standardizing words and pictures" full of pietism, hate and fear of migrants. See "Ali in the City. Contemporary migration patterns: drifts and destinations" (Festival dei Popoli 2015) and "Looking for Neverland" (Festival dei Popoli 2016), www.festivaldeipopoli.org/en (last accessed 13 November 2018).

[6] Migrant cinema remains a rather controversial notion. It has two major definitions: (1) films made by non-European filmmakers; and (2) European films dealing with migrant themes, characters and issues. In this essay we focus on Italian documentary films made (also) by migrants through a participatory process. For a critical discussion on European and Italian cinema of migrations, "Welcome to Schengenland. Tre cinestorie di ospitalità e colpevolezza" by (De Franceschi 2017, pp. 181–97)).

[7] See Gianturco and Peruzzi 2015 for a study on Italian cinema and migrations. For an interview with Dagmawi Yimer on how to "unlearn racism" through cinema of migrations, (Frisina 2018).

[8] Seasonal workers did not have a right to family reunification. Their status prevented them from renting homes, changing employer and reuniting with their families. In the film *Lo stagionale*, Giuseppe, the protagonist, an Italian migrant, his "clandestine" son and the comrades of the Colonie Libere choose to protest for their rights in Switzerland, against the status of seasonal workers. In 1970, outside the Italian embassy and the federal Swiss Parliament, the fiction of the film met the reality of the documentary and the political actors met the actors of the film.

[9] "I thought that this film could give us Italians the chance to clearly see our condition: a mirror in which we could observe our reflected image and take consciousness of how unjust the conditions we lived in were, exploited day and night, separated from our families" (www.swissinfo.ch/ita/con-gli-occhi-di-alvaro-bizzarri--il-regista-operaio/410812).

their children. Bizzarri's militant cinema was possible thanks to the antifascist political socialization in the film clubs of the *Colonie Libere*[10].

This article explores how participatory documentary cinema has become a way of reacting to racism against migrants and of expressing political solidarity with refugees in Italy. According to Andrea Segre (founder of ZaLab) participatory documentary cinema refers to first person accounts, with the protagonists' close involvement in the construction of the story, no external narrating voice and cinematographic detail to aesthetics and photography.

The militancy of participatory documentarists is first moral, then political, and expresses itself in the constant search for more respectful representations of the subjects of the events that are narrated. Unlike Italian directors of previous generations, Segre and other participatory documentarists working on migrations in Italy are more aware of the limits that their gaze may have on the vicissitudes of others. They seek a more symmetrical relationship with migrants/refugees and they are probably also facilitated by their greater familiarity and daily acquaintances with people of foreign backgrounds (Vanoli 2018, pp. 191–92).

Our paper will introduce the roots of participatory documentary cinema in participatory video (White 2003) and it will argue that the documentary work of ZaLab, Archive of Migrant Memories and 4CaniperStrada is unique in the Italian context, by presenting their most important films. Finally, we will discuss the importance of the process of film-making and the politics of "civil distribution" in this particular way of enacting political solidarity with refugees in Italy.

2. Ten Years of Participatory Cinema with ZaLab and Archive of Migrant Memories

The origin of participatory cinema is linked to the activity of the "Challenge for Change/Societé Nouvelle" (CFC/SN) of the National Film Board of Canada (NFBC), which was born from the 1960s civil rights movement, to denounce and address the roots of poverty and social exclusion, to give voice to those who were marginalized by society and to prevent minorities from becoming victims of government and media stereotypes (Frisina 2013).

The main aim of this program was to promote social change by training community action workers to use video, networking and activating citizens, facilitating communication between the government and local communities of citizens.

The CFC/SN's pioneering role in granting citizens access to media production[11] must be recognized, as it gave different groups of citizens a forum through which they could communicate, organize themselves politically and, if necessary, have their complaints reach public officials. In participatory cinema three "circuits of feedback" (Collizzolli 2010) are sought: first of all, an *internal feedback loop*, whereby the film is projected in the local communities and the protagonists can have some control over the montage (indicating what should be kept/changed); secondly, a *horizontal feedback loop*, whereby the film is shown to audiences that are considered "*similar*", that is as having some affinity with the protagonists, in order to create alliances between citizens; finally, an *external and vertical feedback loop*, by projecting to other audiences and looking for dialogue with "experts" and decision-makers. This way of making cinema allows for the creation of a collective subject and gives social actors a sense that change is possible.

In the last decade, participatory cinema has spread in Italy because it can give back the "*dignità del racconto*", the dignity of the story and control over their self-representation to those who are normally only portrayed, and whose suffering is denied or vice versa made spectacular, as in the case of asylum

---

[10] At the end of the seventies the Colonie Libere organized several courses for "animatori cinematografici" all over Switzerland. The aims were teaching those who would direct the film clubs to analyze the films (deconstruct the mechanisms which could capture the "spettatori-consumatori" "spectator-consumers").

[11] From the mid-1990s the "ethics of access" has made headway, an approach to documentaries which aims to both increase the reflexivity/responsibility of the filmmakers with respect to citizen audiences, and also make audiovisual technology more accessible in order to give back to social actors control of how they are represented.

seekers and refugees (Segre and Collizzolli 2016). Participatory cinema with refugees in Italy has produced not only works that are "cinematic in all respects, but above all ethical (...). Just as Primo Levi asked himself if a man could be treated like that, so the directors of Like a man on earth ask themselves the same" (Cincinelli 2009, p. 278).

According to Gatta (forthcoming), adopting a participatory approach means keeping the focus both on the *product* (a counter-narrative on migrations and on Italy as a post-migratory society) and on the relational *process* between migrants as authors and protagonists of the story and audiovisual professionals and cultural facilitators. Each can reflect on their specific point of view, becoming more aware of their social positions.

The independent and non-commercial distribution of participatory documentaries is built on a wide (around 500 partners in Italy and 800,000 public screenings in the last ten years[12]) and, above all, *active* distribution network: each screening has been "co-organized", which means that someone has asked for it and has involved hundreds people from his/her territory in a public discussion. Small and big associations, schools and universities, congregations, social and cultural centers organized screenings of the films often with the presence of refugees, the protagonists of the stories. In a similar way to how participatory theatre makes things happen (Musarò 2017), participatory cinema has enabled those who are considered inferior (victims to save or suspected criminals to control) to speak up and be heard in the local and wider public sphere.

ZaLab (www.zalab.org) is an association of five film-makers and social workers (M. Aiello, M. Calore, S. Collizzolli, A. Segre, S. Zavarise), who have played a very important role in promoting participatory cinema in Italy. The name of the association is a tribute to Cesare Zavattini (one of the first proponents in the Italian Neorealist movement), because of his democratic ideal of spreading the video camera to any Italian home ("like a sewing machine", see Collizzolli 2010, p. 353)[13]. ZaLab's stories stem from participatory video laboratories which aim to have marginalized people express their own reality and then, for those who so desire, to become authors of documentaries. Since 2006 ZaLab has produced[14] and distributed[15] social documentaries on Mediterranean migrations and migrants in Italy/Europe. In ZaLab's view, even though the number of movies on this issue has continued to grow in Italy in the last decade[16], there is still a strong need to contribute to changing the frame (and policies) on migrations through participatory cinema[17]. In particular, two ZaLab documentaries on refugees have become forms of activism and they are made available for free on streaming every time it is necessary to re-open the debate on Italian migration policies.

---

[12] Stefano Collizzolli, personal communication 9 November 2018.
[13] Commenting on Stefania Parigi's text (2014) on neorealism, the renowned film critic Paolo Mereghetti ("the second lives of neorealism" in La Lettura del Corriere 18 August 2014) claimed that neorealist film-makers' deepest aspiration was "to give aesthetic value to the imperatives of ethics". Ethics is key to the work of participatory video, whilst aesthetics is sometimes sacrificed in order to prioritise social intervention. Nonetheless, Zalab, AMM and 4CaniperStrada share the neorealist project of democratising the image and its social impact (Parigi 2014).
[14] Among award winning documentary films on migrations produced by ZaLab: "South of Lampedusa" "Green Blood" and "Ibi" by Andrea Segre, "Our Best Years" by Stefano Collizzolli and Matteo Calore; and "Limbo" by Matteo Calore and Gustav Hofer. On ZaLab's "narratives of change", see (Ardizzoni 2013).
[15] ZaLab distributed films such as "On the bride's side" by Gabriele Del Grande, Khaled Soliman and Antonio Augugliaro; "Les Sauteurs" by Moritz Siebert, Estephan Wagner and Abou Bakar Sidibé; and, most recently, "Iuventa" by Michele Cinque.
[16] Stefano Collizzolli (personal communication, Padova, 26 September 2018) quoted the data collected through www.cinemaitaliano.info and elaborated by Zalab (gray paper, 2016): in 2006 87 independent documentaries were produced, 25 of which were about immigration, in 2014 560 documentaries were produced, and about 200 of these on the theme of immigration.
[17] Andrea Segre is also the director of three fiction films on migrations: "Io sono Li", "La prima neve" and "L'ordine delle cose". The latter is the most political (https://lordinedellecose.it/pamphlet/ last accessed 9 October 2018) and it contributed to creating an Italian national forum for migrants' right to move through legal channels and to stay in Europe in decent conditions (http://pclodc.blogspot.com last accessed 9 October 2018). The name of the movement derives from the movie "Per cambiare l'ordine delle cose" (i.e., to change the order of things).

The first film, "Like a man on earth"[18] by Andrea Segre, Dagmawi Yimer[19] and Riccardo Biadene (Italy, 2008, 60'; ZaLab with Asinitas onlus/AMM, Archive of Migrant Memories) enacted political solidarity with refugees, breaking the silence on the tragic consequences of the Italy-Libya agreement which was supposed to contrast irregular migrations. The agreement was centered on the request for "*respingimenti*" (push backs) by the Italian state and included lucrative business contracts between the two countries.

Dagmawi Yimer interviewed (in Amharic) eight young Ethiopians who had fled their country, and crossed the desert from Sudan to Libya, in metal containers with no food or liquids. The video camera focuses on their faces, listening to their silences and capturing their emotions through close-ups. In Libya they met brutal officials and prison guards who bought them for 30 dinars and dumped them in overcrowded prison cells without clear indictment for months and years on end. Trucks, prisons, containers, jeeps, and body bags were provided by the Italian government as part of the agreement signed with Libyan authorities in 2008. Yimer's thoughts are left to the voices off-camera (Figure 1). Migrants' stories of acts of violence, torture, and systematic rape contrast mainstream political discourse. In the movie Yimer meets Italian (i.e., then foreign minister Franco Frattini) and European politicians and very calmly poses uncomfortable questions which reveal the hypocrisy and inadequacy of his interlocutors. "Do you know anything about the treatment reserved to the detainees in the Kofhra prison?" D. Yimer asked I. Laitinen (director of Frontex, the European Agency for the Management of Operational Cooperation at the External Borders of the Member States of the European Union). His "diplomatic" answer was: "I do not have the details but I was told that there is much room for improvement". The inhuman politics of Libyan detention centers was renewed with other agreements "to stop irregular migrations" (and new lucrative business) in 2017[20]. The film "Like a man on earth" has been screened in 86 Italian public squares since 2008 and has travelled across Italy for ten years thanks to the requests of many associations, cinemas, theatres, schools, universities, parishes, cultural and social centers. Every screening has been an opportunity to "activate" people on the ground and numerous activists have used the film to involve other citizens in direct actions of solidarity with refugees.

Figure 1. Dagmawi Yimer (Ethiopian) watches Italian news where the journalist states that, thanks to the agreement between Berlusconi and Gaddafi, "the colonial contention has been settled" (still frame, used by permission). The documentary seems to show how this story is part of a *neo-colonial* politics of Italy towards Libya (and of Europe towards Africa).

---

[18] http://www.zalab.org/en/projects/like-a-man-on-earth/ (last accessed 9 October 2018). It was presented at Milano Film Festival in 2008 and it was the winner of SalinaDocFest in 2009 (Vanoli 2018, p. 190).
[19] Dagmawi Yimer was a Law student from Addis Ababa who left Ethiopia because of the strong political repression. After crossing the desert, surviving the violence in Libya, he arrived by boat in Italy. In Rome he took part in the participatory video laboratory ("The desert and the sea", 2007) and he started to film.
[20] On this issue, see https://www.msf.org/libya-open-letter-european-governments-are-feeding-business-suffering (last accessed on 9 October 2018).

The second film, "Closed Sea"[21] is by Andrea Segre and Stefano Liberti (Italy, 2012, 60′; ZaLab)—who met their witnesses in Shousha refugee camp (at the border between Libya and Tunisia) and in two reception camps for asylum seekers (C.A.R.A.) in southern Italy. It showed the nexus between "push back operations" and human rights violations against migrants (escaping mainly from Eritrea and Somalia). The European Court of Human Rights in Strasbourg condemned Italy[22] and the documentary contributed to assigning Italian political authorities the responsibility of human rights violations against asylum seekers, providing migrant testimonies in the case of Hirsi Jamaa and Others v. Italy (Palladino and Gjergji 2016).

Italian participatory cinema with refugees is closely linked to another ten-year-long experience, AMM-Archive of Migrant Memories (http://www.archiviomemoriemigranti.net). It was developed in 2007, starting from an organization (Asinitas onlus) engaged in teaching Italian as a second language in creative ways (i.e., involving migrants and asylum seekers in participatory video laboratories, in collaboration with ZaLab). Dagmawi Yimer was one of the founders of AMM. Triulzi (2012) suggested that AMM open a space to share memories of migrants, asylum seekers and refugees with the goal of rethinking Italy with its colonial legacies. AMM's primary interest is promoting the listening of migrants' self-narratives through different tools: textual, audiovisual, exhibitions[23] and, above all, by using participatory cinema, as with "C.A.R.A. Italia"[24] by Dagmawi Yimer or "Welcome to Italy"[25] by Aluk Amiri, Hamed Dera, Hevi Dilara, Zakaria Mohamed Ali and Dagmawi Yimer, who attended a laboratory by Renaud Personnaz (from www.ateliersvaran.com).

Among AMM productions there are "diaries of the return" to Lampedusa. "Nothing but the sea" by Dagmawi Yimer, Giulio Cederna and Fabrizio Barraco (Italy, 2011, 49′) is about the return of D. Yimer to Lampedusa with a video camera and a regular identity card. In 2006 Yimer could only imagine Lampedusa, as he looked through the gratings of the windows of a detention center, but a few years later he met the residents and expressed his gratitude. When undocumented migrants land in Lampedusa they remain confined behind high walls, staying separated from the island and its inhabitants. The film includes moments which have a strong poetic resonance (inspired by the work of the documentarist Vittorio De Seta, according to O'Healy 2012) and reveals how two solitudes, two marginalities can meet. The film gives dignity to its protagonists. Taking up again O'Healy analysis (2012, p. 138), both the *Lampedusani* and the migrants are racialized by the Italian state. In the film a resident of Lampedusa says to Yimer "Before the discrimination against Africans, there was discrimination against Italians from the South". In addition, he adds that Lampedusa is only ever cited by newspapers to talk about the *sbarchi*, that is the boat arrivals, while the problems of the island itself (i.e., the drastic lack of social services) are systematically ignored.

The comparison with other cinematographic views on the island is striking, especially with the most famous, the Berlin award-winning "Fire at sea (Fuocoammare)" by Francesco Rosi (2016), which ends up reinforcing the dominant humanitarian and securitarian frame on migrations, making refugees "poor victims" with no possibility to interact with Lampedusani in more symmetrical ways[26]. The cinematography of "Fire at sea" is very beautiful, but its aesthetics seems detached from politics. To quote Sou (2017, p. 2), "there is a near total erasure of refugees' voices, personal identities and histories. Scenes which feature refugees (re)produce familiar scenes of distressed and desperate groups of black bodies being rescued, cared for, or processed by Italians (...). In contrast, the film

---

[21] http://www.zalab.org/en/projects/closed-sea/ (last accessed on 9 October 2018).
[22] http://unipd-centrodirittiumani.it/en/news/The-European-Court-of-Human-Rights-condemns-Italy-for-its-push-back-policy-to-Libya-in-2009/2381 (last accessed on 9 October 2018).
[23] For example, AMM organized an exhibition with objects of migrants and, more recently, there has been a project with migrants' multimedial diaries (project DIMMI).
[24] http://www.asinitas.org/?portfolio=c-a-r-a-italia-3 (last accessed on 9 October 2018). Per un'analisi di "C.A.R.A. Italia", see O'Healy 2012, pp. 136–7.
[25] http://www.archiviomemoriemigranti.net/en/films/amm-productions/benvenuti-in-italia-welcome-to-italy/.
[26] See also the criticism from the collective Askavusa: https://askavusa.wordpress.com/2016/02/24/1428/ (accessed on 9 October 2018).

is dominated by the personal stories and experiences of Lampedusa residents (...). The audience ultimately learns more about a romanticized identity of the island and its residents at the expense of the hundreds of refugees who are filmed as mass movements of silent, voiceless, and identity-less bodies".

After Yimer's "Nothing but the sea", Zakaria Mohamed Ali—a young Somali journalist- returns to Lampedusa and recalls his stay in the Centre for Identification and Expulsion, searching for lost memories with his video camera ("To whom it may concern"[27], Italy, 2013, 16′).

AMM (co)produced some other films by Yimer: "Va' Pensiero. Walking stories" (Italy, 2013, 55′)[28] on the experiences of three persons who survived racist violence (in Milan Mohamed Ba was knifed in 2009, while in Florence Mor and Cheikh were shot in 2011); "Asmat-Names" (Italy, 2015, 17′ 23″)[29] on the disaster that occurred on 3 October 2013, off the coast of Lampedusa (Figure 2).

Figure 2. Names of people without bodies, meaningful names (i.e., Selam/Peace or Tesfaye/My Hope) of migrants who lost their lives crossing the Mediterranean ("Asmat" still frame, used by permission).

3. 4Caniperstrada: Participatory Cinema with Refugees in Sardinia

4Caniperstrada is an artistic collective of independent photographers, film-makers and social researchers[30] that produces reportages, documentary films and visual research where photography and video-making become tools for social inquiry, observation and representation of contemporary phenomena. The project was born "on the road"—hence the group's name—through the interaction with territories, people, and their stories, focusing mainly on social issues: migration, human rights, human geography, social change.

In ten years of activity the collective has produced several documentary films of an ethnographic/anthropologic nature, organized thematic festivals, as well as meetings with authors and directors, cinema, and photography workshops. They have created an international network of organizations working in the field of visual culture, human rights and cinema and promoted projects aimed at describing social changes by building close ties with territories and local communities.

For several years they have been conducting projects on the language of participatory cinema, giving workshops and producing films together with refugees and asylum seekers in Sardinia, with the intention of creating new cinematographic narratives on biographies and subjectivities within migratory paths.

Sardinia, an island in the middle of the Mediterranean Sea, has seen the number of asylum seekers grow since 2013, and is now hosting over seven thousand migrants. The phenomenon of the reception and flow of forced migrants has opened a great debate on social change on the island.

---

[27] https://vimeo.com/77179552 (last accessed on 9 October 2018).
[28] http://va-pensiero.org See also its anti-racist educational kit edited by AMM, https://www.giuntiscuola.it/lavitascolastica/magazine/news/eventi/percorsi-di-antirazzismo-in-classe-ecco-il-kit-va-pensiero/ (last accessed on 9 October 2018).
[29] https://vimeo.com/114849871 (last accessed on 9 October 2018).
[30] S. Muresu joined the artistic collective since 2007 collaborating as director and visual researcher in workshop of participatory cinema and social documentaries. http://www.4caniperstrada.org/en/productions/ (last accessed on 9 October 2018).

Farms in inland areas or ex-hotels on the coasts are some of the places where the first reception centers were born, thus triggering, often in small communities isolated from the presence of foreigners, a mix of generations, religions, languages, and customs.

The time required for processing asylum requests in Italy (often around 1–2 years) and the continuous denials of the Territorial Commissions to grant refugee status, have prolonged the time spent by migrants in reception centers. All this has led to unprecedented cultural exchanges that Sardinia, in its condition of insularity, had never known before.

Between 2014 and 2017 4CaniperStrada carried out research on the use of participatory methods to produce films (short films and feature films), thus experimenting, together with refugees and asylum seekers, original languages, and horizontal creative processes. This methodology entailed opening the direction to a multi-voiced dialogue and recognizing empathy and subjectivity as distinctive elements of a process where there was no written plot, but only the stories encountered at different stages of a shared emotional, existential, and normative journey. In 2016 they created the first web platform entirely dedicated to participatory cinema in Sardinia, which collects all the workshops and experiences from the field[31].

The two films produced through workshop activities and using the participatory method are:

- *Nako—The Land*[32] (ITA, 2016, 30′), direction of K. H. Beyla, L. Manka, Ali A. Hashi, within the project Video Partecipativo Sardegna[33],
- *On the Same Boat*[34] (ITA, 2017, 71′) direction of Stefania Muresu, T. Khalifa, U. Aziz, S. Suwareh, produced by Roda Film e 4CaniperStrada.

The approach used in the creative process of both films focused on long periods of production and research (on average between one and three years), the centrality of the relationship with the people involved, the spontaneity of contents and narrative choices, searching for co-authorship.

They attempted to break the classic documentary cinema tradition, born together with anthropology and visual ethnology, where filming was seen as a tool for objective documentation of reality. In this way, they experienced the limits of this traditional approach and at the same time they also differentiate themselves from the specific current called "Accented Cinema"[35] made exclusively by migrant directors.

In the following case studies, we explain how the filming practice with refugees was used as a research tool to experience visual forms of dramaturgy of reality: by learning and questioning the way to manage the cinematographic narration during the creative process. The main feature of this experience was the creation of a mixed gaze between refugees and film-makers. This approach also asserts the importance of a "temporary present" (for example the limbo of reception centers) that produced the different forms of re-writing and representation of the other in the two case studies.

Participatory cinema of 4CaniperStrada has been based on low production costs, flexibility, use of non-invasive cameras and handy cams to practice cinema without technical limits, a small crew of 3–4 people, within the idea of a "stylo camera" (Astruc 1948, p. 33), free and able to portray with images and do so with many hands, in a constant dialectics and practice of reflection.

The experience of the two participatory films opens up to the idea of a trans-cultural cinema (McDougall 2015, p. 340), made up of interactional dynamics of observation, of mixed directions and the search for an aesthetic performativity, halfway between the dimension of the process and the

---

[31] http://www.videopartecipativosardegna.net (last accessed on 9 October 2018).
[32] http://www.4caniperstrada.org/en/portfolio/nako-la-terra-nako-the-land/ (last accessed on 9 October 2018).
[33] http://www.videopartecipativosardegna.net (last accessed on 9 October 2018).
[34] http://www.4caniperstrada.org/en/portfolio/on-the-same-boat/ (last accessed on 9 October 2018).
[35] "Accented cinema" comprises different types of cinema made by exilic, diasporic, and postcolonial ethnic and identity filmmakers who live and work in countries other than their country of origin. The distinction between the sub-categories of exilic, diasporic and postcolonial ethnic films is based chiefly on the varied relationship of the films and their makers to existing or imagined homeplaces (Naficy 2001).

cinematographic product. These are works capable of providing a contemporary representation of stories of migrations through new narrative languages, where *"the cinema that belongs to the real, is made in reality and with the real, a large open laboratory, within which critical sense, ethical discourse and the search for truthfulness of the representation converge"* (Dottorini 2013, pp. 16–18).

Nako—The Earth was shot at a reception center in the province of Nuoro, a former agri-tourism business in the agro-pastoral context of Sardinia, geographically isolated from urban settlements.

The protagonists were asylum seekers between the ages of 18 and 25, coming from Sub-Saharan African countries (Gambia, Guinea, Ivory Coast, Mali, Ghana) and Somalia. Circular meetings were organized to provide an introduction to the camera, mutual interviews, activities on geographic maps, and the creation of story-boards. The contents gathered consist of personal stories, discursive interviews, transpositions of cultural concepts in fictional scenes, self-representations, stories related to agricultural work and the land. The geographic isolation and the daily life around the rural environment (the forest) influenced the production of contents in Nako (from the mandinke "garden, field"), which is structured in three micro-stories (*Laboureur et ses enfants, Nabiaulu, Dhulka—The Land*). The film introduces new codes and stratified meanings (in terms of editing choices and poetry of cinematography) to the social truthfulness that the film intends to tell (Figure 3).

By participating in the video-editing, the protagonists reorganized the images shot in narrative terms, thus constructing a dramaturgy of reality and conveying the contents with ethnographic elements typical of their culture of origin and visual perception[36].

The film was disseminated in the local public sphere, in meetings with the participation of the inhabitants, institutions and refugees, now invested with a new role and an artistic experience that allowed them to escape from forced isolation to the edge of the inhabited area. The internal feedback loop started with a first projection in the reception center and then in the small city of Sarule (NU), co-organized with the Municipality and the local school. The aim was to strengthen the relations between the refugees and the local community.

After that, the film went through the horizontal, external, and vertical feedback loops. *Nako-The Land* has also been screened in academic contexts, schools, and thematic meetings as an educational and informative tool. At the cinematographic festival Tertio Millennium, in 2017 the film received an award from Il Cinematografo[37], in the film contest "A Corto d'Identità".

Figure 3. Ali (Somalia) observes the Sardinian landscape, remembering his faraway land. A frame of *On The Same Boat*, a hut in the woods is built, an emotional representation of a journey.

---

[36] Reclaiming or Constructing? Real or Un-Real? How do objective and subjective visions coexist in the places of the image? Definition of "Un-Real" by Giovanni Festa (Dottorini 2013, pp. 51–61): "a sore wound inflicted in the real, embedded in its surface. A reality that raves, disintegrates, imagines".

[37] "A corto di identità" First film prize promoted by Fondazione Ente dello Spettacolo, during Tertio Millennio Film Fest 2017.

On The Same Boat was born as a project for the production of a documentary film. It collects the subjective stories of the life and travel of refugees who arrived from the sea and find themselves in a reception center (CAS) on the beach, in a former tourist resort in northern Sardinia.

The film combines different narrative levels: documentary of reality, interviews, participatory video, and fiction. Filmed between 2014 and 2016 and produced at the end of 2017, it has been presented—as a collaborative film—in several international film festivals, screenings in cultural circuits and in the autumn of 2018, it will travel to other countries (including Africa) thanks to its selection at a festival promoted by the International Organization for Migration.

The protagonists are a young Syrian, two Gambians and a Pakistani co-director, who recounts life in the reception center and the wait for asylum with a sort of candid-camera technique. The center housed over 300 male migrants from various geographical areas (Africa, Pakistan, Bangladesh).

The film observes the daily routine between the center, the beach, and the bar of the small coastal town, until the protagonist meets a boat, metaphor and real *matter* of the film, which reveals the memory of the trip. The narrative form tries to minimize distances and, with poetical empathy (acquired through the long research process) and the use of black and white photography (color is used only for mobile phone images documenting the travels of the migrants), it tries to create a connecting thread between the spectator and the voice of the protagonists.

The video camera is visible, participating, the intent to tell one's story evident and conscious. The gaze is directed to the viewer the images create an emotional relationship between place—memory—character, in a construction of the scenes that is always linked to the complex subjectivity of the protagonist and which interrogates the spectator without granting presumed truths.

The documentary is characterized by a fictional part[38], the construction of a hut in a wood made of reeds and plastic, which from the very beginning is called "home", a transposition into images of Sulayman Suwareh's personal biography, co-author of the film. This inner story of the film was directed and interpreted by Sulayman, starting from his own three-year experience in the Gourougou mountain (on the border between Morocco and Spain, Melilla). The place where he lived and slept—his home—was a hut of plastic in the wood together with hundreds of migrants, which in the film was re-constructed. As an example of the above-mentioned "accented cinema"—the story of the hut has a narrative structure designed by Sulayman, that identifies topic, language (mandinka), a visual style and plot with a personal sensibility (such as the scene where they prepare a tea on the fire *"as we make in Gambia, our country"*).

On The Same Boat, which has been projected mostly through an *external feedback loop* at a cinematographic festival (focused in documentaries and human rights) and a national screening, is today an instrument with which the protagonists become bearers of their artistic project and their migratory experience in Italy. For some of them, participation in the film, presentations during public screenings and collaboration with 4CaniperStrada has facilitated obtaining a residence permit and provided the opportunity to demonstrate their social integration in the host country.

In 4CaniperStrada's experience of participatory cinema, they sought to make a representation based on refugees' visual self-narration, by exercising what Glissant (2005) defines as the "right to opacity" or "that right not to be totally understood and not to totally understand the other" (Massari 2017), a complexity that resists the demand for transparency and exhibition, and which produces critical knowledge and a shared collective heritage created together with migrants, detached from the logic of institutionalized recognition[39].

---

[38] Or ethno-fiction? An example of the use of a language located between cinematographic fiction and a reality developed through the practice of visual ethnography. A definition of ethno-fiction comes from visual anthropology and is provided by the ethnologist and anthropologist Marc Augé: "a narration that evokes a social reality, observed through the subjectivity of an individual", (Augé 2011, p. 8).

[39] María Lugones writes: "through traveling to other people's worlds" we discover that there are "worlds" in which those who are the victims of arrogant perception are really subjects, lively beings, resistors, constructors of visions, even though

4. Conclusions

As the sociologist Emmanuel Ethis (2018) stated, *cinema* not only reveals fragments of the real that the public can accept and recognize, but—to cite Pierre Sorlin—it enlarges the domain of the visible and offers new interpretive frames on a reality. Cinema can have a social impact in different ways: offering alternative values to the mainstream; allowing spectators to identify with people and situations that they are not familiar with; and finally enthusing and drawing on people's emotions to motivate them to take action. Called on by the film, the spectators may feel compelled to "respond" (Sorlin 1977).

Italian participatory documentary cinema with refugees has been our privileged point of departure from which to explore how it is possible to challenge the mainstream narrative of migrations in Europe and to promote new forms of everyday interactions between locals and refugees in Italy.

The Italian documentary cinema presented in this article has been made with refugees through a participatory process of film-making and by adopting a politics of "civil distribution".

The participatory process has allowed the viewers to appreciate the positive force of migrants' active testimony (O'Healy 2012, p. 139) which warns the audience of how framing refugees as victims entails downplaying their dignity and the ability to take charge of one's own life. Moreover, changing point of view thanks to refugees' memories has helped to rethink Italian history. For instance, Dagmawi Yimer refers to Italian colonialism in Ethiopia at the beginning of "Like a man of Earth" as "the first time our great grandparents (Italian and Ethiopian) met"; Aboubakar (in "C.A.R.A. Italia") tells Dagmawi: "Our grandparents told us that Italians were good people, that they knew them; our ears heard this and we came to Italy. When we arrived we found something else".

ZaLab, AMM and 4CaniperStrada have given Italian audiences the opportunity to reconnect with their past and to learn how to feel "responsible" (etymologically, "able to give a response") in the present. For instance, AMM has committed to working above all in schools and universities within reflective, antiracist programs in which young people are encouraged to write a "collective diary" where they weave the direct testimonials of refugees through the audiovisual and their own stereotypes which they collectively discuss. Several times the discussions after the films quoted in this article have ended with a "call for action" at a local level. For instance, the activists of Baobab Experience (https://baobabexperience.org) have organized screenings with ZaLab films and every time they have found new volunteers to support refugees in Rome.

Italian participatory documentary cinema has thus become a form of enacting political solidarity with refugees, involving citizens in local direct social actions and in different forms of protest (i.e., symbolic actions to denounce social injustice in the governmental reception system). DVDs with ZaLab's documentaries -such as "Like a man of earth" and "Closed sea"—were sent to many Italian politicians as a "Christmas gift" by citizens in campaigns dedicated to assigning political authorities[40] the responsibility to open legal channels of migration and to change the negative social conditions of asylum seekers and refugees in Italy. The text of the campaign[41] was sarcastic, calling for helping politicians who live in "a dramatic condition of ignorance" to know the consequences of their decisions.

In recent years, film-makers from ZaLab, AMM and 4CaniperStrada have paid increased attention to the product, to reach a wider audience and to promote advocacy campaigns for migrants and refugees' rights. This shift seems to be even more necessary today, when symbolic and physical violence against migrants and refugees appears legitimated by the political discourse of the new Italian government and, especially, by the Home Office Minister Matteo Salvini (from the xenophobic

---

in the mainstream construction they are animated only by the arrogant perceiver and are pliable, foldable, file-awayable, classifiable", (Lugones 1987, pp. 3–19).

[40] Here there are the first 50 Italian politicians who received this gift: http://comeunuomosullaterra.blogspot.com/2008/12/politici-natale-come-un-uomo.html.

[41] About 45,000 people joined the campaign and more than 150 dvds were sent as gift to politicians from Italian citizens (Stefano Collizzolli's personal communication, 26 November 2018).

party "Lega Nord"). Participatory cinema keeps on playing an important role to enact a political solidarity with refugees[42] in difficult times not only for the System of Protection for Asylum Seekers and Refugees (SPRAR)[43], but also in a more general crisis of Italian democracy, by inviting citizens to challenge the new faces of fascism (Traverso 2017) through the arts of de-bordering.

Author Contributions: A.F. wrote the Introduction, the Section 2. Ten Years of Participatory Cinema with ZaLab and Archive of Migrant Memories and the Conclusions. S.M. wrote the Section 3. 4Caniperstrada: Participatory Cinema with Refugees in Sardinia.

Funding: This research received no external funding.

Acknowledgments: The authors wish to thank Gabriel Tzeggai, Dagmawi Yimer, Stefano Collizzolli, Gianluca Gatta, Francesca Helm and Leonardo De Franceschi.

Conflicts of Interest: The authors declare no conflict of interest.

References

Ardizzoni, Michela. 2013. Narratives of change, images for change: Contemporary social documentaries in Italy. *Journal of Italian Cinema & Media Studies* 1: 311–26.
Astruc, Alexandre. 1948. The birth of a new avant-garde: the caméra-stylo. In *Journal L'Écran Français*. Paris: Peter Graham.
Augé, Marc. 2011. *Diario di un Senza Fissa Dimora. Etnofiction*. Milano: Raffello Cortina Editore.
Barisione, Mauro. 2009. Comunicazione e Società. Teorie, Processi e Pratiche del Framing. Bologna: Il Mulino.
Cincinelli, Sonia. 2009. *Immigrati nel Cinema Italiano*. Bologna: Edizioni Kappa.
Collizzolli, Stefano. 2010. Il Video Partecipativo: dalla Comunicazione Sociale alla Socializzazione della Comunicazione. Ph.D. dissertation, University of Padova, Padova, Italy, January 10. Available online: http://paduaresearch.cab.unipd.it/2443/1/il_video_partecipativo._Dalla_comunicazione_sociale_alla_socializzazione_della_comunicazione._Il_caso_di_ZaLab.pdf (accessed on 15 November 2018).
De Franceschi, Leonardo. 2017. *Lo Schermo e lo Spettro. Sguardi Postcoloniali su Africa e Afrodiscendenti*. Milano: Mimesis.
Della Porta, Donatella, ed. 2018. *Solidarity Mobilizations in the 'Refugee Crisis'*. Contentious moves. Basingstoke: Palgrave.
Dottorini, Daniele. 2013. *Per un cinema del reale. Forme e Pratiche del documentario italiano comtemporaneo*. Udine: Forum.
Ethis, Emmanuel. 2018. *Sociologie du cinéma et de ses publics (4e éditions)*. Paris: Armand Colin.
Fassin, Eric. 2010. *La Raison humanitaire. Une histoire morale du temps présent*. Paris: Seuil.
Frisina, Annalisa. 2013. *Ricerca visuale e trasformazioni socio-culturali*. Torino: UTET Università.
Frisina, Annalisa. 2018. Disimparare il razzismo attraverso il cinema? Dialogando con Dagmawi Yimer. In *Visualità e (anti)razzismo*. Edited by InteRGRace. Padova: Padua University Press.
Gatta, Gianluca. forthcoming. Autonarrazione e antirazzismo nelle pratiche didattiche dell'Archivio delle Memorie Migranti. In *Imago migrantis: migranti alle porte dell'Europa nell'era dei media*. Edited by V. Tudisca, A. Pelliccia and A. Valente. Roma: CNR-IRPPS e-Publishing.
Gianturco, Giovanna, and Gaia Peruzzi. 2015. *Immagini in movimento: lo sguardo del cinema italiano sulle migrazioni*. Reggio Emilia: Edizioni Junior.
Glissant, Eduard. 2005. *Poetica della relazione*. Macerata: Quodlibet.
Iervese, Vittorio. 2016. Altro che invisibili. Il paradosso delle immagini. *Zapruder*, 130–39.
La Barba, Morena. 2018. Cinema, migrazioni e antirazzismo: un percorso nella Svizzera dei Trenta Gloriosi, in InteRGRace (a cura di), Visualità e (anti)razzismo. Padua University Press. Available online: http://www.padovauniversitypress.it/system/files/attachments_field/9788869381201.pdf (accessed on 15 November 2018).
Lugones, María. 1987. Playfulness. "World"-Travelling, and Loving Perception. *Journal Hypatia* 2: 3–19. [CrossRef]
Massari, Monica. 2017. *Il Corpo degli altri, Migrazioni, memorie, identità*. Napoli-Salerno: Orthotes.
McDougall, David. 2015. *Cinema Transculturale. Nuoro: ISRE*. Princeton: Princeton University Press.

---

[42] In 2018 ZaLab organized a one-year project in collaboration with SPRAR, using participatory video laboratory to engage both refugees and social workers involved in the reception system, from North, Centre and South Italy.
[43] Minister Salvini's recent "decreto immigrazione" has dramatic effects on migrants' rights and on the system of reception of asylum seekers and refugees. See https://www.meltingpot.org/Il-CdM-ha-approvato-il-decreto-immigrazione-ma-la-battaglia.html#.W6-TwmW3m0g (last accessed 9 October 2018)

Musarò, Pierluigi. 2017. The Art of De-Bordering.How the Theater of Cantieri Meticci Challenges the Lines Between Citizens and Non-Citizens. In *Performative Citzenship: Public Art, Urban Design, and Political Participation*. Edited by Laura Iannelli and Pierluigi Musarò. Milano: Mimesis International.

Naficy, Hamid. 2001. *An Accented Cinema: Exilic and Diasporic Filmmaking*. Princeton: Princeton University Press.

O'Healy, Aine. 2012. I documentari dei migrant. In *Quaderni del CSCI*. Barcelona: Quaderni del CSCI, pp. 134–39.

Palladino, Mariangela, and Iside Gjergji. 2016. Open 'Hearing' in a Closed Sea. Migration Policies and Postcolonial Strategies of Resistance in the Mediterranean. Interventions. *International Journal of Postcolonial Studies* 18: 1–18. [CrossRef]

Parigi, Stefania. 2014. Neorealismo. In *Il nuovo cinema del dopoguerra*. Venezia: Marsilio.

Ponzanesi, Sandra. 2011. Europe in motion: Migrant cinema and the politics of encounter. *Social Identities* 17: 73–92. [CrossRef]

Segre, Andrea, and Stefano Collizzolli. 2016. Il racconto condiviso. Zalab, video partecipativo e richiedenti asilo. In Quaderni del Servizio Centrale, pp. 49–56. Available online: https://www.sprar.it/wp-content/uploads/2016/06/Documenti/Quaderni_servizio_centrale/Quaderno_Teatro_rifugiati.pdf (accessed on 15 November 2018).

Snow, David A. 2004. Framing Processes, Ideology and Discursive fields. In *The Blackwell Companion to Social Movements*. Edited by David Snow, Sarah Soule and Hanspeter Kriesi. Oxford: Blackwell Publishing, pp. 380–412.

Sorlin, Pierre. 1977. *Sociologie du cinema*. Paris: Aubier.

Sou, Gemma. 2017. Fire at Sea (Fuocoammare) directed and produced by Gianfranco Rosi (Italy 2016, 114'). *The Journal of Nationalism and Ethnicity* 46: 1–2.

Traverso, Enzo. 2017. *I nuovi volti del fascismo*. Verona: Ombre Corte.

Triulzi, Sandro. 2012. Per un archivio delle memorie migranti. *ZAPRUDER 28, maggio-agosto 2012* 28: 120–25.

Vanoli, Giancarla. 2018. *Nella terra di mezzo. Cinema e immigrazione in Italia 1990–2010*. Milano: Meltemi.

White, S. A. 2003. *Participatory Video: Images that Transform and Empower*. London: Sage.

Zamponi, Lorenzo. 2018. From border to border: Refugee Solidarity Activism in Italy across space, time and practices. In *Solidarity Mobilizations in the 'Refugee Crisis'*. Contentious moves. Edited by Donatella Della Porta. Basingstoke: Palgrave, pp. 99–123.

© 2018 by the authors. Licensee MDPI, Basel, Switzerland. This article is an open access article distributed under the terms and conditions of the Creative Commons Attribution (CC BY) license (http://creativecommons.org/licenses/by/4.0/).

Article

Refugees for Refugees: Musicians between Confinement and Perspectives

Hélène Sechehaye [1,*] and Marco Martiniello [2,*]

1. Faculté de Philosophie et Sciences Sociales, Musicologie, Université libre de Bruxelles, 1050 Brussels, Belgium
2. Fund for Scientific Research-FNRS and Faculty of Social Sciences, Liège University, Bâtiment 31 Boîte 24 Quartier Agora—Place des Orateurs, 3, 4000 Liège (Sart-Tilman), Belgium
* Correspondence: hsecheha@ulb.ac.be (H.S.); m.martiniello@uliege.be (M.M.)

Received: 26 November 2018; Accepted: 7 January 2019; Published: 16 January 2019

Abstract: Driven by the solidarity movements following the "refugee crisis" of 2015, the Brussels-based non-profit organization Muziekpublique, specialized in the promotion of so-called "world music", initiated the *Refugees for Refugees* project. This album and performance tour featured traditional musicians who had found asylum in Belgium and had artistic, political, and social goals. In comparison to the other projects conducted by the organization, each step of the project benefited from exceptional coverage and financial support. At the same time, the association and the musicians were facing administrative, musical, and ethical problems they had never encountered before. Three years after its creation, the band *Refugees for Refugees* is still touring the Belgian and international scenes and is going to release a new album, following the will of all actors to go on with the project and demonstrating the important social mobilization it aroused. Through this case study, we aim at questioning the complexity of elaborating a project staging a common identity of "refugees" while valuing their diversity; understanding the reasons for the exceptional success the project has encountered; and determining to what extent and at what level it helped—or not—the musicians to rebuild their lives in Belgium.

Keywords: refugees; diversity; migration; world music; fair participation

---

1. The "Migrant Crisis" in Brussels

By the end of summer 2015, the "migrant crisis"[1] reached new dimensions in Europe and shook public opinion (Georgiou and Zaborowski 2017). Belgian political authorities did not adapt quickly enough to receive migrants who were arriving on their territory: hundreds of them,[2] as they were waiting to fill in their asylum application at the Foreigners' Office, were staying in the nearby Parc Maximilien in Brussels.[3] In this tense context, numerous solidarity and humanitarian initiatives flourished.[4]

Several actors in the cultural sector, whose activities do not specifically concern refugees, decided to contribute in their own way. The radio station *Musiq'3* set up the project "Musiques d'exil" ["musics

---

1. Also referred to as "migrants' crisis" by the media, or "welcome crisis" in the more engaged media (for an analysis of the lexical treatment of the event, read Calabrese 2018).
2. The estimated figure varies between 600 individuals (Wahoud Fayoumi, "Réfugiés à Bruxelles: "Jamais je n'aurais imaginé un camp en Belgique" [Refugees in Brussels: "I'd never have imagined a camp in Belgium"], rtbf.be [online], 9 September 2015) and 1200 (Thomas Mangin, "Parc Maximilien, le village pour réfugiés s'organise tant bien que mal" [Parc Maximilien, the village for refugees is getting organized as best it can], Le Soir [online], 16 September 2015).
3. This problematic situation has not ended with the so-called "welcome crisis": in 2018, hundreds of migrants are still gathering around the Parc Maximilien where they sleep at night, or are taken care of by associations.
4. September 2015 saw the birth of the non-profit organization *Plateforme Citoyenne de Soutien aux Réfugiés Bruxelles* [Brussels Citizen Platform for Refugee Support], which coordinates all the initiatives and is still active three years later [http://www.bxlrefugees.be/en/ seen 8 August 18].

of exile"];[5] *Syrians Got Talent* was created to send a "strong political message of solidarity and for social inclusion."[6]

In this article, we will discuss an initiative led by the Brussels non-profit organization Muziekpublique, which "defends and promotes musics of the world"[7] by organizing concerts, coordinating a music school, and producing CDs.[8] In October 2015, Muziekpublique launched the *Refugees for Refugees* project[9] to record an album featuring refugee musicians, whose purpose was both artistic, political, and social. Each step was marked by exceptional media coverage and financial support compared to the other projects run by the organization.[10] The CD was even awarded *Best album of 2016* by the Transglobal World Music Charts. At the same time, the association and the musicians faced administrative and ethical problems they had never been encountering before. As a former Muziekpublique's employee, Hélène Sechehaye coordinated the project from inside the organization from 2015 to summer 2016, and then continued to have regular contacts with the project. This article is largely based on her work during that period.

We aim at understanding the reasons for the exceptional success the project encountered in the cultural, associative, and media worlds. We will also discuss the ambiguity of this process that develops a common identity of "refugees" while simultaneously valuing their diversity. Finally, we will try to determine whether the project has modified or not the individual trajectories and the migratory careers (Martiniello and Rea 2014) of the musicians involved? To what extent and at what level did it help—or not—the musicians to rebuild their lives in Belgium?

2. Refugee Musicians, Bearers of Attacked Traditions

The analytical methods applied to musical practices in migratory context are of growing interest, having first emerged in the Anglo-Saxon world,[11] and recently reached the French-speaking academic world.[12] These studies often focus on the activity of minorities within urban societies, on diversity and multiculturality about western cities subject to globalization (Stokes 2004; Vertovec 2009; Aubert 2011; Bouët and Solomos 2011; Martiniello 2014; Devleeshouwer et al. 2015). In this context, Élina Djebbari's study of a "transcultural" project identifies the two directions of application: one in which "hybridization is established as a norm", the other advocating "the promotion of identities (where it is considered that the original musical style must remain identifiable, despite the mixing" (Djebbari 2012, p. 10). The concept of "diversity" is handled by the Belgian political world in the 21st century (Observatoire des Politiques Culturelles 2013, p. 4) to legitimize its public policies—even if what becomes a value is far from being shared by all segments of the population. Moreover, cross-cultural projects involving diversity are sometimes criticized for their "substantialization"[13] of cultures (Zask 2014), as well as for their representation of a form of diversity that would be "acceptable", and "aseptic" (Sainsaulieu et al. 2010, pp. 103–12).

---

[5] Achille Thomas, "Musiques d'exil: le Festival Musiq'3 lance un projet de soutien aux réfugiés" [Musics of exile: Musiq'3 Festival launches a project to support refugees], *Musiq'3*, 2 February 2016 [https://www.rtbf.be/musiq3/emissions/detail_festival-musiq3/accueil/article_musiques-d-exil-le-festival-musiq-3-lance-un-projet-de-soutien-aux-refugies?id=9203019&programId=3773 seen 24 August 2018].

[6] Description of the project on their Facebook page *Syrians Got Talent* [https://www.facebook.com/pg/SyriansGotTalent/about/ seen 24 August 2018].

[7] About this controversial designation, read (Aubert 2005, 2011; Bachir-Loopuyt 2008; Bouët and Solomos 2011; Olivier 2012).

[8] Organization's description on their website [https://muziekpublique.be/about/?lang=en, seen 24 August 2018].

[9] Band's website [http://muziekpublique.be/artists/refugees-for-refugees/ seen 18 September 2018].

[10] Interview with Peter Van Rompaey and Lynn Dewitte, Brussels, 28 February 2018 [our translation].

[11] To name a few: (Stokes 1994; Baily and Collyer 2006; Zheng 2009; Levi and Scheding 2010; Bouët and Solomos 2011; Pistrick 2015; Martiniello et al. 2009; ...).

[12] Several research projects are being carried out in Nanterre and Saint-Étienne (Damon-Guillot and Lefront 2017); the 2018–2019 nomadic seminar of the French Society of Ethnomusicology is entitled "Music and immigration in France"; the next issue of the *Cahiers d'Ethnomusicologie* will be devoted to "Migrants' Music". We can also mention Martiniello et al. (2009).

[13] Substantialization of culture, sometimes called "essentialization" (Capone 2004; Djebbari 2012) is defined by Zask as follows: "a particular culture as a kind of unified whole that customs have fixed on the one hand, history and circumstances on the other. Ethnicity then appears as an index of fixity", a stable entity hermetic to change that would stick to the skin.

"Integration" is often used along with diversity in policy and public debates. Whereas it indicates "social, political, cultural and economic processes that occur when migrants arrive in a new society" (Martiniello 2006, p. 4), it is often thought of as a linear process leading from the "migrant" status to the "integrated" foreigner, without considering potential stops or steps back. To nuance it, Martiniello and Rea (2014) propose the concept of "migratory careers", that implies status changes as well as identity changes at each step of the career, breaks with the linear path concept and the migration/integration dichotomy. Martiniello proposes to replace integration with the term *fair participation*, that concerns "target individuals and groups in the social, economic, cultural and political spheres of the host European societies. In this perspective, a satisfactory level of immigrant integration is achieved when immigrants have similar participation patterns than non-immigrant citizens." (Martiniello 2006, p. 9).

Can we approach refugees' musical practices as usual migrants' practices? There is a lack of literature on the music of refugees, who are specific migrants since the musical life of their country of origin is difficult if not destroyed, and as they have no possibility of returning to their country of origin.[14] The definition of the object "refugee" is also problematic, because this status can be mobilized by people who do not possess this recognition but consider themselves as belonging to the "refugee" group, like Afghan individuals who were told by the Foreigners Office that the place they escaped is on the "safe areas list" and therefore cannot be granted the status legally (Tahri 2016).

Lambert (2018) notes that cultural heritage in the countries of origin is endangered by the destruction of archives, concert halls, the hunt for musicians and the exile of populations. Tahri (2016, p. 102) emphasizes the role that music, as poetry or dance, can play in "promoting the well-being of refugees". Several studies have been carried out in migrant camps (Öğüt 2015; Tahri 2016; Emery 2017) and/or within specific communities (Diehl 2002; El-Ghadban 2005; Öğüt 2015). Most studies present these musical practices as part of the transit migration: musicians in refugee camps are not intended to settle there and are often on their way to other places. This influences their musical practices: "The feeling of being "unsettled" restricts the social and cultural relationships that can be formed with the local culture" (Öğüt 2015, p. 273). Though, Capone (2004, p. 11) notes that almost any deterritorialization process is followed by a re-territorialization process.

While it seems difficult to leave aside the problematic concept of "community" in ethnomusicology (Salzbrunn 2014), the "refugee" category encompasses heterogeneous populations in terms of nationality, religion, language ... Therefore, we will here use the *event lenses* and study the different actors gathered by a particular event, rather than the *ethnic lenses*, which would focus on a particular social group defined with reference to ethnicity not relevant in the framework of this project.

3. *Refugees for Refugees*, from the Idea to the Stage

2.1. A Musical Metaphor

Muziekpublique launched the production of *Refugees for Refugees*, an album featuring refugee musicians living in Belgium. Its aim was and still is simultaneously artistic, political, symbolic, and social: to bring the voices of refugee musicians to the media through an album while helping them to integrate in European professional networks. Peter Van Rompaey, director of Muziekpublique, sets the context:

> The purpose of our label is to support artists to develop their careers from A to Z. Here, the initial aim was to show that among refugees there are very good musicians, to show an

---

[14] The "refugee" status may be withdrawn from an individual who has been granted it if he or she travels to his or her country of origin. Source: General Commission for Refugees and Stateless Persons, leaflet "Vous êtes reconnu réfugié en Belgique. Vos droits et vos obligations" [You are recognized as a refugee in Belgium. Your rights and obligations], November 2016, p. 10. Available online: https://www.cgra.be/sites/default/files/brochures/2016-11-25_brochure_reconnu-en-belgique_fr_0.pdf (accessed on 16 October 2016).

image of refugee artists as a metaphor that they are also doctors, chemists . . . All refugees have talents, they are not items to reject.[15]

The first exchanges around the project raised questions about the composition of the band: which "refugees" did the project want to feature? Muziekpublique eventually decided to follow its usual artistic line and to work with high-skilled musicians from classical and popular traditions, located in Belgium. As musicians were in a precarious situation, the decision was made to produce the album in a very short time:[16] the speed made it also possible to guarantee media attention since the issue of refugees was a top media priority. The project was called *Refugees for Refugees* because part of its profits would be donated to social organizations promoting refugees' expression, well-being and fair participation through amateur artistic practice.[17]

To find musicians, Muziekpublique contacted its usual artistic networks, but also organizations working in the associative field.[18] Four artists simply refused to take part in the project, and three withdrew later for various reasons:[19] the conditions of the recordings did not suit them;[20] they could not find time to play music between administrative interviews, training, professional and family obligations. Some others expressed doubts about the project itself, first because its aims and results were very unclear when they were contacted, but also because many musicians were reluctant to be labelled as "refugees".

In one month, a very heterogeneous group was brought together, made of some twenty musicians from different countries,[21] sometimes speaking no common language,[22] arrived by different means and having various legal statuses [Figure 1].

As the recordings began, this heterogeneity also became a musical problem: how to combine various repertoires, musical systems, and languages? Muziekpublique looked for a musical mediator and director they already knew to coordinate the project. After a Syrian 'ūd player they had proposed refused to play this role, they eventually asked the Belgian 'ūd player Tristan Driessens, experienced in conducting transcultural ensembles.

---

[15] Interview with Peter Van Rompaey, Brussels, 30 August 2018 [our translation].
[16] Seven months separated the first discussion on the project from the CD release: the search for musicians began in October 2015, funding requests were sent in November, recordings took place in December 2015 and February 2016, and the CD was released in May 2016.
[17] Two Brussels non-profit organisations, *Globe Aroma* and *Synergie 14*, are given 1€ each per CD sold.
[18] Humanitarian organizations, welcome centers, language schools for newcomers, and citizen initiatives.
[19] Unfortunately, due to the poor conditions in which the collaboration stopped with these musicians, they did not wish to answer the questions asked in the context of this article, probably no longer wishing to be associated with it.
[20] Muziekpublique, not having large resources, proceeds for this project as it does for others: the recordings take place in "live" conditions and not in a studio; some musicians, thinking they will be included in a full classical orchestra, realize that they can only work with the musicians on board; the association cannot provide accommodation for musicians coming from far away during the recordings period.
[21] Syria, Iraq, Pakistan, Afghanistan, and Tibet. Despite the non-recognition of their country on the official level, the musicians participating in the project consider themselves as "Tibetans". Muziekpublique then chose to indicate this geographical area at the same level as the other nations in the description of the project, a militant choice that sometimes prevented the project from being programmed for important institutional events.
[22] While lack of language skills is generally not an obstacle, Muziekpublique used translators on several occasions: during initial contacts with musicians; or during major conflicts involving members of the band.

Figure 1. *Refugees for Refugees* during the CD release concert (Muziekpublique, Brussels, 13 May 2016). On stage: 17 musicians from 8 countries playing 15 different types of musical instruments and singing in 3 languages. Among them: 5 asylum seekers waiting for a decision, 8 having obtained the administrative "refugee" status, 3 Belgians, 1 stateless person. Credits: Jean-Luc Goffinet and Muziekpublique (used by permission).

Looking for financial support also happened to be faster than usual. Needing a start-up capital, the association used crowdfunding for the first time, which met and even exceeded its objective.[23] An interest was also felt on the institutional side: the European Commission provided a support budget; the Wallonia-Brussels Federation, normally not entitled to support musicians not residing legally on its territory—which was the case of the majority of the group's musicians—granted an exceptionally high budget for the recording of the album.

Simultaneously, the mainstream media, usually not much interested in world music, paid particular attention to the project.[24] Several articles and major programs were devoted to *Refugees for Refugees* before the release of the album:[25] this interest would never decrease.[26] The project coordinator Lynn Dewitte, also regrets that it was not directed towards the musical project for itself but rather towards its political dimension and the musicians' personal stories:

---

[23] €15.755, 126% of the initial goal, were collected in one month thanks to 272 supporters.
[24] The week of the recordings in December 2015 was a real media marathon.
[25] "Des réfugiés unis par la musique" [Refugees united by music], *La Libre Belgique*, 14 December 2015; "The Musician from Diyala", *Al Jazeera* (UK), 24 December 2015; "Tout le Baz'Art" [The whole baz'Art], *Arte/La Trois*, 1 March 2016; "Les Festivals de musique ouvrent leurs scènes aux artistes réfugiés" [Music festivals open their stage to refugee artists], *Télérama*, 22 June 2016; "De la musique en mémoire d'Alep" [Music in the memory of Aleppo], *Le Soir*, 21 April 2016; "Virtuoze vluchtelingen" [Virtuoso refugees], *De Standaard*, 13 May 2016; "L'Invitation" [The invitation], *RTBF—La Trois*, 16 May 2016.
[26] Recently "Des réfugiés jouent pour les réfugiés, au gré des marées" [Refugees play for refugees, at the discretion of the tides], *Le Monde*, 16 August 2018; "Quand on est sur scène, je ne sens pas que nous sommes réfugiés" [When we are on stage I don't feel we are refugees], *Libération*, 21 August 2018.

Journalists have preconceived ideas that they want to include in their articles. However, musicians do not necessarily want to get involved politically, sometimes they do not want to hear about politics anymore: their commitment is in music.[27]

This exclusive commitment in music was confirmed by Tammam Ramadan, a musician in the project:

On stage, we break down [religious, linguistic] barriers, while there are wars at these borders. [...] It costs nothing, it's the cheapest solution. I hope we can replace wars with music, because it's more effective.[28]

However, tensions were palpable during the months preceding the CD release. Some musicians left the project because it did not meet their musical and professional expectations. The choices that the production team had to make concerning the layout of the album and its cover (Figure 2) raised questions of representation: the cover picture did not represent the whole band, and an imbalance was felt in the distribution of the tunes—some musicians would have liked to play on more tunes for instance.[29] In the end, the musicians hardly identified themselves with the final product.

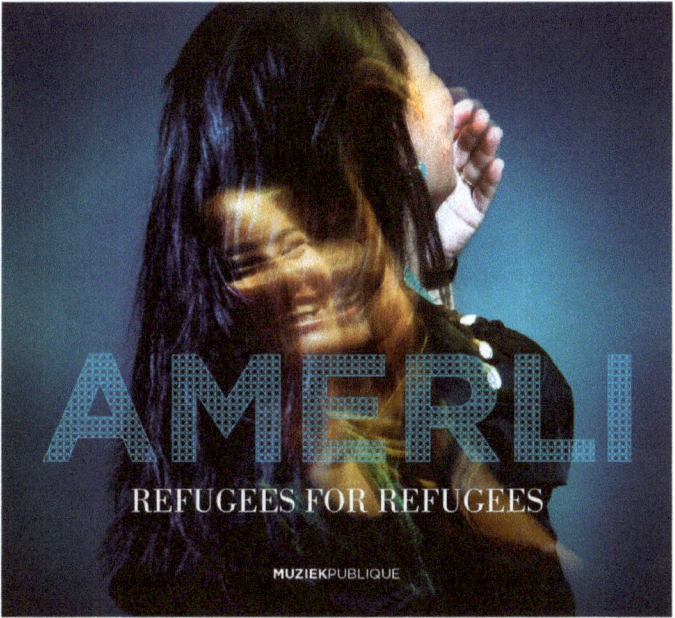

Figure 2. The cover of the album shows the Tibetan singer Dolma Renqingi. *Amerli*, the title of the CD, refers to an Iraqi city. Credits: Dieter Telemans, Desiree de Winter & Muziekpublique (used by permission).

The album's release concert in Brussels, on 13 May 2016 in the theatre Molière, the home of Muziekpublique, was crowded with world music aficionados, curious individuals, and several associations supporting migrants, who came with groups of their recipients.

---

[27] Interview with Lynn Dewitte, Brussels, 30 August 2018 [our translation].
[28] Interview with Tammam Ramadan, Brussels, 30 August 2018 [our translation].
[29] Which was not feasible: for various reasons, at no time could all the musicians get together. Similarly, the photo sessions were not attended by all artists.

2.2. From Song Compilation to Stage Performance

The band was quickly asked to give performances[30], and musicians were enthusiastic to play some more concerts together. For technical and financial reasons, the band had to be reduced to ten musicians:[31] the choices, made in a logic of scenic production, focused on the variety of profiles and repertoires, on the musicians' ability to play together as well as on their desire to get involved in a long-term professional project in Belgium. While the band included musicians of various nationalities, several requests concerned a "band of Syrians" in relation to recent arrivals of refugees in the country.[32]

Muziekpublique also faced unusual demands. Many music festivals oriented towards "world music"[33] wanted to feature *Refugees for Refugees*, whose musical repertoire is rather to be included in the category of "traditional music"[34].

> I usually don't feel that our project is different from the others, because we play in the same places than the other Muziekpublique's projects. But sometimes there have been festivals where, when I saw the other bands, I wondered if they had invited us just for the name of our band, because you feel that the music in these festivals is not the same as ours",[35] says Tammam Ramadan.

Other types of solicitations came from more official institutions. The presence of *Refugees for Refugees* was intensely desired but little valued in practice; for instance, the band was sometimes used as background music during a buffet.[36] When the band was awarded the Culture Price by the Flemish Commission, it was proposed to take part in the ceremony and play some 15-s jingles before the announcement of each laureate, behind a curtain. After negotiations, the band also played two whole songs in front of the audience.

Many requests from the volunteer sector concerned events intended for their users, often refugees, to show them that some refugees have "successful" trajectories, willing to share with them positive stories as well as the opportunity to spend a festive moment with familiar music. The wage proposed to artists was often very low: while *Refugees for Refugees* tended to integrate musicians professionally, the fact that they needed to be paid decently to pursue their life project did not always seem to be a main concern for those who wanted to book them for a show.

In the end, the variety in the proposals was not necessarily perceived positively by Peter Van Rompaey:

> We are of course happy that the project works. [...] But we have the feeling that for this project, it is the theme that attracts. As it is in the news, the programmers jump on it without

---

[30] Even before the CD was released, the band was invited by the *Music Meeting* (Nijmegen, NL), *Festival de Wallonie* (Villers-la-Ville, BE), *Espéranzah!* (Floreffe, BE), Festival Les Suds (Arles, FR), *Festival d'Art de Huy* (BE) and *Les Rencontres Inattendues* (Tournai, BE).

[31] At its beginning, the band was gathering Ali Shaker Hassan (*qānūn*), Aman Yusufi (*dambura* and vocals), Asad Qizilbash (*sarod* and violin), Dolma Renqingi (vocals and choreography), Kelsang Hula (*dramyen* and vocals), Khaled al-Hafez (vocals and *daf*), Simon Leleux (*darbūka*), Tammam Ramadan (*nāy*), Tareq al-Sayed Yahya ('*ūd*) and Tristan Driessens ('*ūd*). Today, Souhad Najem (*qānūn*) has replaced Ali Shaker and Fakher Madallal (vocals) has replaced Khaled.

[32] Since 2015, the main nationalities of asylum seekers have changed: while Syrians still arrive in large numbers in Belgium, new migrant groups are now mainly made of Eritreans and Sudanese people.

[33] In French as well as in English, the "world music" label generates much confusion. Laurent Aubert (2011, p. 32) established three categories encompassed by this term: folklore music, world music and traditional music. According to him, the label "world music" refers to fusion repertoires: "experiences generated by the meeting of musicians from diverse backgrounds and by the integration of "exotic" instruments and sounds into the electronic equipment of current Western music production" (Aubert 2011, p. 33, our translation).

[34] Music with an acoustic aesthetic, oriented towards the act of listening and often perceived by Western audiences as "authentic", unlike *world music*, which fully assumes an aesthetic of hybridity (Aubert 2011, p. 33).

[35] Interview with Tammam Ramadan, Brussels, 30 August 2018 [our translation].

[36] This made the Aleppo musicians particularly angry: they refused to play their Sufi repertoire in front of an audience drinking alcohol that was not even listening to them.

even listening to the songs, just because the musicians are refugees. We would like our other projects to generate the same interest.[37]

2.3. Musicians on Tour: Work, an Obstacle to Fair Participation?

While all the musicians in the band eventually obtained a legal status in Belgium,[38] many have since been affiliated to the CPAS[39] and face enormous difficulties in getting paid. The musician's work irregularity does not allow the CPAS to establish a protocol. Every month, problems concerning contracts, postpone the reception of money and cause many difficulties.

The CPAS system also sets a maximum earnings ceiling: above a given amount, the musicians' wage is deducted from their monthly allowance.[40] A feeling of uselessness to work may be felt, and even more, sometimes a musician who spends money for his transport or the babysitter cannot receive additional financial compensation, and must therefore indirectly "pay" to work.[41]

Things are not easier for the few musicians who decide to enter the labor market by accepting non-artistic work: fixed working hours make it difficult to spend several days abroad.

> "The difficulty of their situation is one of the things that does not change. Even with so many concerts [...] One of the musicians had managed to leave the CPAS and was trying to make a living from classes and concerts, but after two years he gave up, it was too hard," says Lynn Dewitte.[42]

However, some have been able to highlight their involvement in music as a positive point to advocate their case with the administration, as Tammam Ramadan explains:

> When the CPAS employees asked me to find a job, they thought music was my hobby, and proposed me to work as a vegetable cutter in a restaurant. Showing them my contracts helped me to defend my artistic project.[43]

Two particular barriers to a professional career were mentioned.[44] On the one hand, travelling outside the Schengen area is difficult for people with the status of refugee[45]. Although this situation has not yet occurred, it is a potential problem.[46] On the other hand, the family situation, and the events in their country of origin disrupts the musicians a lot, even if they do not talk about it at work. In these conditions they find it difficult to devote themselves totally to their artistic production. Yet, the *'ūd* player Tristan Driessens, notes that music can sometimes ease injuries:

> Sometimes, there are musicians who carry on their shoulders very heavy bereavements [...] Being able to express oneself in Europe through one's instrument, one's art, makes it much lighter.

---

[37] Interview with Peter Van Rompaey, Brussels, 30 August 2018 [our translation].
[38] When they arrive in Belgium, asylum seekers must submit a file to the CGRS (Office of the commissioner general for refugees and stateless persons). In the time period preceding the granting or not of refugee status, asylum seekers are in a precarious legal status, legally not allowed to work in Belgium.
[39] CPAS (Centre public d'action sociale [Public social action center]): in Belgium, a public institution that supplies a number of social services including a monthly allowance for those who do not have a job or access to unemployment benefit.
[40] These ceilings vary according to the allowance received and the CPAS to which they are affiliated.
[41] The application of these laws differs from one CPAS to another, and even within the same CPAS, a general lack of clarity surrounds the recipients' rights. As on this FAQ from Brussels City CPAS website: "*Do I still have the right to earn money if I receive the living wage?* It depends on the case: it is imperative to inform your assistant of any amount of money received". The assistant in question is available on a permanent basis one hour a week, during which the phone line is saturated with calls. Source: "Some frequently asked questions". Available online: http://www.cpasbru.irisnet.be/fr/index.asp?ID=66 (accessed on 27 August 2018) [our translation].
[42] Interview with Lynn Dewitte, Brussels, 30 August 2018 [our translation].
[43] Interview with Tammam Ramadan, Brussels, 30 August 2018 [our translation].
[44] Interviews with Lynn Dewitte and Peter Van Rompaey, Brussels, 30 August 2018 [our translation].
[45] Two of the musicians held Syrian passports that were expired. Moreover, the Syrian passport is not eligible to travel so some countries, like in Morocco where the band could not take part to a big world music festival.
[46] Since the Syrian embassy in Belgium is considered functional again, musicians are required to renew their passports, but are reluctant to support financially and symbolically a regime from which they had to flee.

It always creates an atmosphere of joy despite the realities that are still there […] I witness how music can really heal pain and suffering.[44]

3. Three Years Later: Same Name, New Shape

In two years, the band *Refugees for refugees* gave about sixty concerts and the album sold more than 2500 copies.[48] While some tensions are still present, the musicians became used to each other's musical languages and are now driven by the desire to progress together. The idea of a new album, presenting the "work of the band," has gained ground. An important turning point in the band's life was an artistic residency in the fall of 2017, during which new compositions were thought for the whole group, musical textures were worked on. The band really became a band, and was no longer the addition of individuals. A balance was found between the different repertoires, but the main focus is still on the bridges created between them. "The moments of exchange between the repertoires are what people [from the audience] appreciate most," says Lynn Dewitte.[49] The description of the project now highlights the message of hope and resilience conveyed by the project, as well as the album turns a new page, symbolizing reconstruction.[50]

The relevance of the designation *Refugees for Refugees* is questioned: as seen above, the denomination of musicians as "refugees" is sometimes experienced in a negative and stigmatizing way. Hussein Rassim, *'ūd* player who was involved in the early stages of the project, says in this regard:

> Once the sadness of no longer playing with the band passed, I realized that it opened up other opportunities for me. During a festival in Tournai, I played on the same stage than *Refugees for Refugees*. But while their names were appearing in small, under the project title, mine was appearing in large. I realized that my career could also take advantage from it.[51]

This name will finally be maintained so that professionals recognize the continuity of the project. Tammam Ramadan says: "After four years in Belgium, you have to understand that you are a refugee, whether you agree or not."[52]

The new CD release, no longer considered as a separate project but as an ordinary production of Muziekpublique, is scheduled for February 2019. Artistically, all the participants are convinced that it will be musically better than the previous one, but doubts are expressed about the same warm welcome as for the first opus, because "[the subject of refugees] is not so fashionable anymore."[53]

4. Refugees' Narratives, Skills, and the Music

The *Refugees for Refugees* project stands out from the other projects supported by Muziepublique. First thought of as a one-shot project, it received particular attention in terms of funding, by the media as well as the audience. Gradually, it has changed and has developed in the long run, responding to a demand from some musicians, Muziekpublique and other organizations. Aiming at promoting and networking high-skilled musicians who arrived in Belgium, *Refugees for Refugees* differs from other projects born during the "welcome crisis" by its longevity and by the repertoire played by the musicians—a repertoire that comes from "back home" (Emery 2017, p. 57). In the discussion,

---

[44] Interview with Tristan Driessens for "La Musique, moteur d'émancipation" [Music, the engine of emancipation], RTBF 26 December 2017 (9'40). Available online: http://www.youtube.com/watch?v=fs8eqTMLsSY&t=36s (accessed on 18 September 2018).
[48] Figures provided by Muziekpublique on 31 August 2018.
[49] Interview with Lynn Dewitte, Brussels, 30 August 2018 [our translation].
[50] Description on the crowdfunding website Available online: https://www.kisskissbankbank.com/en/projects/refugees-for-refugees-new-album (accessed on 30 December 2018).
[51] Interview with Hussein Rassim, Brussels, 6 September 2018.
[52] Interview with Tammam Ramadan, Brussels, 30 August 2018 [our translation].
[53] Interview with Peter Van Rompaey, Brussels, 30 August 2018 [our translation]. The present seems to prove him right: at the time of writing, a crowdfunding launched by the association for the production of the band's second CD is struggling to achieve its objective.

we will examine to what extent it affects cultural, social, economic, and political aspects of the refugees' presence in Belgium.

4.1. To Be a "Refugee" Musician, between Confinement and Perspectives

In the beginning of the project, the musicians we asked to fit in a top-down approach that values their differences, turned towards the substantialization of their musical practices (Zask 2014). Each one played a repertoire from his or her home country. This approach of diversity through world music was described by ethnomusicologist Laurent Abert as such:

> In a multicultural environment such as that of the major Western metropolises, one can notice that *world musics* represent both unifying standards of identity and bridges between communities; they are one of the few areas in which the integration of each individual does not imply assimilation to dominant models (Aubert 2011, p. 28 [our translation]).

One could first wonder what would be the musical dominant model in Belgium, what kind of musical models would musicians be expected to assimilate? Their own musical traditions and heritage are either *exoticized* or neglected. It certainly is difficult for them to navigate between these two scenarios or to find another way to participate and be recognized by the Belgian music world and by the larger society.

However, it seems that the visibility is made easier by adhering to the simplistic categories in which musicians are classified without further reflection (Cabot 2016, p. 20). While one of the project's aims was to show the diversity present within this "refugee" band, the framework seemed to imply a way of featuring it that leaves little space for negotiation.

This approach is then perceived as locking up: Hussein Rassim, who founded his own band, reports that the organizers who contact him are surprised that there are also Belgian musicians in his band, while they would have preferred only "refugees."[54] Similarly, some criticism has been leveled at Muziekpublique regarding the presence of two Belgian musicians in a band of so-called "refugees". The arrival of immigrant and refugee populations, which has led to policies and discourses on "living together" that aimed at building bridges, has paradoxically led these same actors to build barriers by identifying and institutionalizing distinct categories of people (Observatoire des Politiques Culturelles 2013, p. 14).

The epistemological violence carried by the term "refugee" also raises the issue of refugees considered as voiceless, deprived of their agency, who could only speak when given the word (Cabot 2016). It is interesting to note that, as long as it fit the musical quality required, Muziekpublique did not interfere in the repertoire played by the musicians. Roles were distributed clearly: Muziekpublique was responsible for the production work, and the musicians for the repertoire. It resulted in the fact that some musicians sometimes did not agree on the ways the project was introduced; or that Muziekpublique discovered that a new song with what they considered as unbearable kitsch arrangements had appeared during a concert. But overall, this way of working allowed the project to emerge and progress despite the different perspectives of about thirty participants.

Although the project was part of the news, fighting with mainstream discourses against refugees hosting, it did not aim at being sensationalist. The musicians' journey and suffering were not recounted unless asked by journalists. In the music of the album, all musicians were not willing to speak about their suffering and escape. Spiritual Sufi songs follow traditional songs praising Epicureanism; poems remembering Himalayan mountains; or an instrumental evoking the epic of a city besieged by the Islamic state[55]. If the refugee narratives implicitly appear along the album, the musicians did not make

---

[54] Interview with Hussein Rassim, Brussels, 6 September 2018.
[55] This last piece, despite being the only one to explicitly refer to the reasons which made the musician escape—or precisely by that virtue—became the title song of the album ("Amerli").

it its common theme: songs with sometimes opposing speeches rub shoulders, echoing the musicians' various profiles.

Gradually, from a project featuring "art by migrants", the project has transformed itself into a "transcultural creation" (Djebbari 2012), "mobilizing its cultural differences as its conscious object" (Appadurai 2001, p. 206) to raise awareness both to the various traditions brought by refugees, and to the bridges that can be built between them. The ensemble transformed itself into a band with which the musicians can identify, with a unified discourse around their musical practice. Despite the band's name, their art is not about migration or about migrants anymore: their approach is touched by "migratory aesthetics" (Bennett 2011) mainly because the experience of migration allowed their encounter, their discovery of other musical languages, their project together.

The CD encountered an obvious success: it was awarded "World Music album of the year" by the *Transglobal World Music Charts* in 2016;[56] it received the Culture Prize from the Flemish Community in 2017; international media praised it (*Al Jazeera*; *Froots*; *Songlines*; *BBC*; *Le Monde*; *Libération* ...). Programmed all over Europe, the band got a warm welcome in every place where it performed. Despite the fact that the musicians cannot physically travel to their home countries, digital distribution of the album and social networks reached an audience worldwide. Proudly[57] sharing the project news on their Facebook page, the musicians received hundreds of expressions of support from their compatriots. This transnational dimension of the *Refugees for Refugees* project is not the focus of this article, but it seems clear that people seeing their own musical cultures endangered in their countries tend to support initiatives maintaining these musical cultures elsewhere.

Cabot (2016) shows how refugee voices are often silenced even—or particularly—when they are "given a space of speech"—this last expression already denying them any autonomous speaking. We saw that though communication was clearly oriented, the content of the album was totally left to the artists, resulting in songs about love, religion, politics, nature ... After all the events described earlier—organizers asking for the project without having heard a song; music used as a background for banquets—one could ask who really listened to the music? These pieces are not of exile, but the words that musicians themselves wanted to say.

Some interesting self-reliance demonstrations happened unexpectedly—or not—outside the project. During the first year after the CD release, Tibetan singer Dolma Renqingi developed some musical projects featuring rock and pop repertoires. Without claiming that there is a direct link with *Refugees for Refugees*, we can assume that taking part to this project gave her confidence and tools to mobilize networks she had newly acquired in Belgium. Another musician of the band ran for the municipal election for the first time in 2018: again, without knowing if there is any causal link to this,[58] we could suppose that playing with musicians from other backgrounds, having to cope with new language and administrative challenges, and juggle networks is something that could have been reinforced through his involvement in *Refugees for Refugees*.

Muziekpublique's inability to meet some of the musicians' demands lead to some big conflicts and sometimes leavings. These departures were firstly felt as failures, but have actually led some musicians to express their agency by creating their own artistic project.

4.2. A Project Based on Skills

Among the remaining musicians, several of them joined the European professional networks through this project—which would probably have happened anyway for most of them, but at a slower

---

[56] Transglobal World Music Charts website. Available online: http://www.transglobalwmc.com/charts/best-of-2016-chart/ (accessed on 4 September 2018).
[57] Although out of reach of this article, it should be noted that "these aspects of pride should be taken seriously" (Cabot 2016, p. 18).
[58] We unfortunately did not have any interview with him about his political investment and therefore do not know if he is running for reasons related to migration, artistic or other issues.

pace. In the end, leaving the CPAS system remains difficult for several of them; being paid for playing their music also remains difficult, despite the fact that they have been working on this project for almost three years. With few exceptions, the administrative situation of artists has not dramatically changed; and the band still faces difficulties in travelling outside the Schengen area.

Muziekpublique targeted the self-reliance of musicians, wishing to go beyond the representations of "refugees" as victims and vulnerable (Refugees Studies Centre 2017) by presenting them as skilled people. Their wish for autonomy seems to have partially failed, at least in economic terms, as Peter Van Rompaey expresses:

> Their situation is still complicated, even if they have a good time [during the concerts]. It's very difficult to move on to another level, and it's perhaps the biggest disappointment ... But it's the same [...], it's not just about being a refugee musician. It's hard to play music from your own country and to be accepted by the mainstream media. Somewhere along the line, it's the biggest disappointment, not only about this project. The organizers are interested in the history of the musicians, but in reality, few are interested in what they do.[59]

The lack of flexibility of the institutions, the administrative uncertainty and lack of knowledge of the necessary tools seem to be structural reasons preventing the empowerment of musicians or in other words to take full control of their migratory and musical careers.

> "In addition to providing livelihoods, projects for refugees, humanitarian and political actors should address the systemic issues, such as barriers to work or a lack of legal representation, that create challenging work and living conditions for refugees" (Refugees Studies Centre 2017, p. 2).

This brings us to the refugees' narratives: whereas one cannot criticize the advantages of going beyond the representation of refugees as victims, representing them as super-refugees (high-skilled individuals or heroes) can also influence badly our perception of refugees who do not meet these expectations (Fiddian-Qasmiyeh 2017). This question was central to Muziekpublique's concern, whose explicit main goal is artistic—proposing quality to a demanding audience, whereas working with refugees or other musicians.[60] What would happen to the "non-chosen" ones? Muziekpublique answered this question in two ways. On the one hand, some of the projects founded by refugee musicians who were not enrolled in *Refugees for Refugees* have been set into Muziekpublique's regular programing.[61] On the other hand, by helping financially organizations whose work with refugees is based on an amateur artistic practice, Muziekpublique indicates and supports the many ways in which music can take part in helping refugees. This situation induces a small reversal in which seems one-way. The musicians are not only hosted in Belgium: by contributing with the donation of a part of the CD profits to other associations, they have closed the loop and become hosts of other refugees.

Several ethical issues are also raised by this project. The selection procedure for musicians, conducted by the association, favored word of mouth and networks, and did not reach all the refugee musicians living in Belgium. The participants were lucky enough to be in the right place at the right time. Second, Muziekpublique's efforts to find musicians only allowed them to meet three female musicians, among which only one stayed in the band, the singer Dolma Renqingi.[62] The representation of women is a recurrent question in the world music worlds as in other artistic worlds (Zheng 2009, p. 41; Olivier 2012, p. 58; Pouchelon 2014, p. 207). Not being very present on stage, they are

---

[59] Interview with Peter Van Rompaey, Brussels, 30 August 2018 [our translation].
[60] We do not have the opportunity to tackle this issue in the limited framework of this article, but Laborde (2012) illustrates the various ways of being considered as a professional world musician.
[61] *Qotob Trio* 6 October 2017; *Wajd Ensemble* 24 August 2017 and 13 October 2018; *Nawaris* 27 January 2018; *Damast Duo* 13 October 2018 ...
[62] Of the other two musicians, one left the project because she did not accept the precarious recording conditions; the other was a Belgian musician invited to the album.

conventionally confined to the roles of singer or manager. Studies focusing on refugee populations note that women are usually invisible and therefore even more vulnerable than men (Emery 2017, p. 65; Refugees Studies Centre 2017, p. 3). Third, the project coordinators are all Belgians, as is the musical director. With one exception,[63] the refugee musicians hold various non Belgian nationalities. A racialized division of labor (Stokes 2004) can be observed within the project. One our reviewers rightly pointed out that this article used to include more quotes from Muziekpublique's workers than from musicians[64]. Aware of this problem, Muziekpublique tried to make things change from within, and for example hired one of the band's musician to work a part-time administratively for the project.

Have the musicians really benefited from the project? In light of these elements, one might be tempted to assume that in spite of good intentions, *Refugees for Refugees* could be an involuntary reinforcement of a situation this project claimed to fight against (Stokes 2004, p. 372). The association advocates "self reliance" but at the same times intervenes in many ways by deciding decide how to communicate around the project, hiring translators during major conflicts or by the presence of a (non-refugee) musical mediator. At the same time, refugee musicians use their agency to build the repertoire, to change the performance conditions when they do not agree with it, and sometimes leave the project for new horizons.

Using the term "refugees" in the band's name clearly conditioned its reception by the media and organizations. This status, which was perceived as a stigma by musicians but as the banner of a struggle by Muziekpublique and the media (Devleeshouwer et al. 2015, p. 113), changed with the formation of musicians as a real ensemble. Some musicians were asked if they would have conducted the project differently, particularly with regard to the choice of the name: some replied that they would have found another name, some said that they do not know, and others that they would probably have chosen the same name, for communication reasons. We hope that this section, considering all the nuances and the heterogeneous nature of the individuals gathered by the project, proved the difficulty to simply oppose Muziekpublique and the "refugee" musicians.

5. Conclusion: Can We Talk about Results? A Project Raising Multiple Issues

The initial goals of the project *Refugees for Refugees* were to produce a high quality album; to help refugee musicians to integrate in professional European music networks; and to promote the cultures carried by "refugees" and to change the way they were socially viewed. As these objectives are multiple, so are the results: some of them seem to be fully accomplished, others to have partially—or totally—failed. Our definition of "success" and "failure" must take into account not only an economic point of view, as we should be tempted to do, but also consider the other dimensions such as social and cultural. Another thing to point out is that despite the institutional weight, the ordinary relationships between people, the situations of diversity people face every day go much faster than politics (Vertovec 2009, p. 28).

Given the reviews from the specialized media and the numerous concert proposals, but also the abundant expressions of support from compatriots residing in home countries, the musical quality objective was reached. The evaluation of the second objective is more difficult: if musicians have indeed played on several major European scenes, their participation into the labor market is more or less effective on a case-by-case basis. Few musicians said this project helped them to enter the Belgian market; more face real difficulties to get out of what could be called the vicious circle of social aid. Finally, it is difficult to assess the project's role in looking at the "refugees" issue in Belgium:[65]

---

[63] The percussion player Simon Leleux was hired for his musical skills and his ability to adapt to different repertoires, which no refugee percussionist presented.
[64] After having balanced the whole I analyzed this was due to many factors, among which my own experience in the production; my missing skills in Tibetan, Pashto and Urdu language; the fact that musicians who had left the project did no longer want to talk about it (see above).
[65] More generally, Georgiou and Zaborowski (2017, p. 3) note that the presentation of refugees by the European media has changed in the course of the year 2015. The sympathetic reaction of a large part of the press during the summer and

we do not know how many people have been affected by the project, nor whether they were already convinced by the cause before the project started or whether it really helped to improve the visibility of the refugees' struggle for their rights.

The analysis through migratory careers points out the interest of considering the resettlement of migrants not only through the economic dimension, but also through their social, cultural, and other needs (Tahri 2016; Refugees Studies Centre 2017; Martiniello 2014). The examination of several levels that were influenced by the project helps to reflect the complexity of the situation, evolving at different speeds. The use of music allowed a certain kind of participation into the host society: musicians found their place in a group and the pleasure of playing music; they have had access to a professional activity; and some of them see it as an ideological involvement ("crossing borders on stage"). Music makes it possible to build links "beyond identity" (Bennett 2011, p. 473). It might seem strange that in this article about a musical project, co-written by a musicologist, music is so little mentioned; however, that is finally what this project was all about: moving people with an aesthetic shock.

Nevertheless, the host society in which we would like musicians to *participate fairly* (or "integrate") has structural problems at the root: racism and sexism; overestimation of the activity of "work" even though the professional sector is difficult to access; and considering that work is a major path to participation while there are many others. Moreover, the "othering" of refugees can be identified as an encouragement to substantialize them as "extra-territorials" and thus justify their different treatment by medias, policies, and institutions (Glick Schiller 2010, p. 109). Paradoxically, while work is overestimated in speeches, there is a great disorder in the modes of professional integration for world music artists, whether they are refugees or not (Laborde 2012, p. 11). If musicians and their projects are symbolically valued by society, there is a need for another form of institutional support that would allow artists to take into account the specificity of their situation—especially when they come to take refuge in a country about which they do not know anything. The bridge between the migratory career and the musical career still needs to be built.

Author Contributions: Writing—original draft, H.S.; Writing—review & editing, M.M.

Funding: This research received no external funding.

Acknowledgments: Heartfelt thanks to the anonymous reviewers and Anne Damon-Guillot for their sharp and precious comments; to Marco Martiniello who took over the supervision as soon as it was needed; to Nastasia Dahuron for her review of the translation; to Stéphanie Weisser whose participation was missed; and to the Muziekpublique team and musicians who work hard to make music happen.

Conflicts of Interest: The authors declare no conflicts of interest.

References

Appadurai, Arjun. 2001. *Après le colonialisme. Les conséquences culturelles de la globalisation [Modernity At Large: Cultural Dimensions of Globalization]*. Paris: Payot & Rivages. First published 1996.

Aubert, Laurent, ed. 2005. *Musiques migrantes, de l'exil à la consécration*. Genève: Musée d'ethnographie.

Aubert, Laurent. 2011. *La musique de l'autre. Les nouveaux défis de l'ethnomusicologie*. Genève: Georg.

Bachir-Loopuyt, Talia. 2008. Le tour du monde en musique. Les musiques du monde, de la scène des festivals à l'arène politique. *Cahiers d'ethnomusicologie* 21: 11–34.

Baily, John, and Michael Collyer. 2006. Introduction and Special Issue, Music and Migration. *Journal of Ethnic and Migration Studies* 32: 11–17. [CrossRef]

Bennett, Jill. 2011. Migratory Aesthetics: Art and politics beyond identity. Directed by Mieke Bal and Miguel A. Navarro Hernandez. In *Art and Visibility in Migratory Culture: Conflict, Resistance, and Agency*. Amsterdam: Rodopi, pp. 450–75.

Bouët, Jacques, and Makis Solomos, eds. 2011. *Musique et Globalisation: Musicologie–Ethnomusicologie*. Paris: L'Harmattan.

---

particularly in early autumn 2015 has gradually given way to mistrust and, in some cases, hostility towards refugees and migrants.

Cabot, Heath. 2016. "Refugee Voices": Tragedy, Ghosts, and the Anthropology of Not Knowing. *Journal of Contemporary Ethnography* 45: 645–72. [CrossRef]

Calabrese, Laura. 2018. Faut-il dire migrant ou réfugié? Débat lexico-sémantique autour d'un problème public. *Langages* 210: 124–5. [CrossRef]

Capone, Stefania. 2004. À propos des notions de globalisation et de transnationalisation. *Civilisations (Bruxelles, Université Libre de Bruxelles)* LI: 22–29. [CrossRef]

Damon-Guillot, Anne, and Mélaine Lefront. 2017. *Comment Sonne la ville? Musiques Migrantes de Saint-Etienne*. Villeurbanne: CMTRA/Université Jean Monnet.

Devleeshouwer, Perrine, Muriel Sacco, and Corinne Torrekens, eds. 2015. *Bruxelles, Ville-Mosaïque. Entre espaces, Diversité et Politiques*. Bruxelles: Editions de l'Université Libre de Bruxelles.

Diehl, Keila. 2002. *Echoes from Dharamsala: Music in the Life of a Tibetan Refugee Community*. Berkeley and Los Angeles: University of California Press.

Djebbari, Elina. 2012. Du trio de zarb aux "créations transculturelles". La création musicale du percussionniste Keyvan Chemirani: Une globalisation parallèle? *Cahiers d'Ethnomusicologie* 25: 111–37.

El-Ghadban, Yara. 2005. La musique d'une nation sans pays: Le cas de la Palestine. In *Musiques—Une encyclopédie pour le XXIème siècle*. Directed by Jean-Jacques Nattiez. Tome 3. Arles/Paris: Actes Sud/Cité de la Musique, pp. 823–52.

Emery, ed. 2017. Radical Ethnomusicology: Towards a politics of "No Borders" and "insurgent musical citizenship"—Calais, Dunkerque and Kurdistan. *Ethnomusicology Ireland* 5: 48–74.

Fiddian-Qasmiyeh, Elena. 2017. Disrupting Humanitarian Narratives? Representations of Displacement Series. Available online: https://refugeehosts.org/representations-of-displacement-series/ (accessed on 29 December 2018).

Georgiou, Myria, and Rafal Zaborowski. 2017. Couverture médiatique de la « crise des réfugiés»: perspective européenne. In *Rapport du Conseil de l'Europe*. Available online: https://rm.coe.int/couverture-mediatique-cirse-refugies-2017-web/168071222e (accessed on 26 November 2018).

Glick Schiller, Nina. 2010. A global perspective on transnational migration: Theorising migration without methodological nationalism. In *Diaspora and Transnationalism. Concepts, Theories and Methods*. Directed by Rainer Bauböck, and Thomas Faist. Amsterdam: Amsterdam University Press, pp. 109–129.

Laborde, Denis. 2012. Faire profession de la tradition? Equivoques en Pays Basque. *Cahiers d'ethnomusicologie* 25: 205–18.

Lambert, Jean. 2018. Les musiques du Moyen-Orient: patrimoines en danger? In *Al Musiqa*. Paris: Éditions La Découverte/Cité de la musique, pp. 73–79.

Levi, Erik, and Florian Scheding, eds. 2010. *Music and Displacement: Diasporas, Mobilities, and Dislocations in Europe and Beyond*. Lanham: Scarecrow Press.

Martiniello, Marco. 2006. Towards a coherent approach to immigrant integration policy(ies) in the European Union. *Intensive Programme "Theories of International Migration"*; Liège: Liège University, August 29. Available online: http://www.oecd.org/dev/38295165.pdf (accessed on 26 November 2018).

Martiniello, Marco, ed. 2014. *Multiculturalism and the Arts in European Cities*. New York: Taylor & Francis.

Martiniello, Marco, and Andrea Rea. 2014. The concept of migratory careers: Elements for a new theoretical perspective of contemporary human mobility. *Current Sociology* 62: 1079–96. [CrossRef]

Martiniello, Marco, Nicolas Puig, and Gilles Suzanne, eds. 2009. Créations en migration, Parcours, déplacements, racinements. *Revue Européenne des Migrations Internationales* 25: 7–11.

Öğüt, Evrim Hikmet. 2015. Transit migration: An unnoticed area in ethnomusicology. *Urban People-Lidé města* 2: 269–82.

Olivier, Emmanuelle, ed. 2012. *Musiques au monde. La tradition au prisme de la création*. Sampzon: Deltour-France.

Observatoire des Politiques Culturelles. 2013. La Diversité Culturelle. Repères. Politiques Culturelles 3. Available online: http://www.opc.cfwb.be/index.php?id=9943 (accessed on 26 November 2018).

Pistrick, Eckehard. 2015. *Performing Nostalgia. Migration, Culture and Creativity in South Albania*. Ashgate: Farnham.

Pouchelon, Jean. 2014. Les Gnawa du Maroc: Intercesseurs de la Différence? Étude Ethnomusicologique, Ethnopoétique et Ethnochoréologique. Ph.D. dissertation, Université de Montréal, Montréal, QC, Canada; Université Paris Ouest, Nanterre, France.

Refugees Studies Centre. 2017. Refugees Self-Reliance. Moving Beyond the Marketplace. In *RSC Research in Brief* 7. Oxford: Oxford University.

Sainsaulieu, Ivan, Monika Salzbrunn, and Laurent Amiotte-Suchet, eds. 2010. *Faire communauté en société. Dynamique des appartenances collectives*. Rennes: Presses Universitaires de Rennes.

Salzbrunn, Monika. 2014. Traverser des paysages sonores translocaux: Réflexions méthodologiques sur la transnationalisation du religieux à travers la musique et les événements. Paper presented at International Conference on the Transnationalization of Religion Through Music, Montréal, BC, Canada, October 16–18.

Stokes, Martin, ed. 1994. *Ethnicity, Identity and Music. The Musical Construction of Place*. Oxford: Providence, Berg.

Stokes, Martin. 2004. Musique, identité et "ville-monde". Perspectives critiques. *L'Homme* 171–72: 371–88.

Tahri, Anissa. 2016. "Je suis réfugié". Entre Affirmation Identitaire et Reconnaissance, le Parcours d'asile des Afghans en Belgique. Master's dissertation, Université Libre de Bruxelles, Bruxelles, Belgium.

Vertovec, Steven. 2009. *Conceiving and Researching Diversity*. Working Paper 09-01 given at Max Planck Institute for the Study of Religious and Ethnic Diversity. Göttingen: Max-Planck Institute, pp. 8–29.

Zask, Joëlle. 2014. Contre "l'identité culturelle" et "l'appartenance", la question de la culturation individuelle. Available online: http://joelle.zask.over-blog.com/2017/04/contre-l-identite-culturelle-et-l-appartenance-la-question-de-la-culturation-individuelle.2014.html (accessed on 26 November 2018).

Zheng, Su. 2009. *Claiming Diaspora: Music, Transnationalism, and Cultural Politics in Asian/Chinese America*. New York: Oxford University Press.

 © 2019 by the authors. Licensee MDPI, Basel, Switzerland. This article is an open access article distributed under the terms and conditions of the Creative Commons Attribution (CC BY) license (http://creativecommons.org/licenses/by/4.0/).

Article

Harnessing Visibility and Invisibility through Arts Practices: Ethnographic Case Studies with Migrant Performers in Belgium

Shannon Damery * and Elsa Mescoli *

CEDEM—Centre for Ethnic and Migration Studies, Faculty of Social Sciences, University of Liege, Bâtiment 31 Boîte 24 Quartier Agora—Place des Orateurs, 3 4000 Liège, Belgium
* Correspondence: Shannon.Damery@uliege.be (S.D.); E.Mescoli@uliege.be (E.M.)

Received: 13 February 2019; Accepted: 1 April 2019; Published: 4 April 2019

Abstract: This paper endeavors to understand the role of arts in migration-related issues by offering insights into the different ways in which artistic practices can be used by migrants and investigating migrants' differing objectives in participating in the arts. Through the exploration of the initiatives of undocumented and refugee migrants involved in artistic groups in Belgium, this paper compares the motivations of the performers and concludes that art can operate as an empowering tool for migrants as it constitutes a space for agency, notwithstanding the specific scope of which it is contextually charged. It allows migrants to render themselves visible or invisible, depending on their contrasting motivations. The creative productions of the first group, composed by members of "La Voix des sans papiers de Liège", a collective of undocumented migrants, corresponds to an explicit effort of political engagement in the local context. The other examples are of undocumented and refugee artists joining musical groups with no specific aim of promoting the cause of undocumented and refugee persons. The choice to be involved in such groups highlights their desire to be, in some ways, invisible and anonymous while participating in this collective of artists. Through these examples, we see that art offers opportunities for migrants to actively participate in the socio-cultural and political environment in which they reside and to claim various forms of official and unofficial belonging whether it occurs through visibility or invisibility.

Keywords: arts; migration; Belgium

1. Introduction

The arts are one of the most accessible conduits through which migrants may find a sense of community belonging, even when not granted any kind of official acceptance or citizenship. Art can be used "to assert dignity and claim national membership" (DiMaggio and Fernández-Kelly 2015, p. 1236). It can be a way to increase 'visibility', raise awareness about a certain situation, further political aims, or to allow one to seamlessly fit into a community and find group belonging when one has no other aim than to become 'invisible'. In this article, we use mainly anthropological and sociological tools (both in terms of methodology and literature) to illustrate what was learned from case studies in arts groups in two urban areas in Belgium. We show how arts practices have been used by migrants to achieve the same aim, that of belonging in Belgium, but in two very different ways. In one case, undocumented migrants claim their right to be in Belgium by promoting their cause and making themselves visible through arts practices, and in the other cases, undocumented migrants and refugees use the arts as a way of blurring boundaries in order to shift their status as 'others' and obtain unofficial belonging in music groups.

As O'Neill (2008) argues, there is tension between the discourse excluding migrants through criminalization, detention, deportation and control of borders, and the discourse that speaks of human rights, responsibilities and possibilities for multi-cultural citizenship. This tension is reflected in the fact that, generally in the media, asylum seekers and refugees are represented by other parties instead of being given the space to represent themselves. Performative arts-based work counters this misrecognition, thus becoming political. The study of these practices through collaborative research methods permits the fostering of mutuality among the researcher and his or her research participants (O'Neill 2008) and highlights the agency of the latter. Migrants have developed alternative and creative strategies for political action because they are excluded from formal means of political participation, such as elections, and from almost all kinds of political decision-making processes (Salzbrunn 2014). Migrants' artistic representations of their own lived experiences can be transformative by providing a conduit for recognition and by allowing migrants to act in a "socially significant way," regardless of their legal status, which May (2013) asserts is key to belonging. Street (2003) analysis of the link between politics and music underlines the ability of music to rally people together and stir an emotional collective response. Music has been used as a tool by governments, political actors, and various groups with political agendas to garner support for causes, but Street also points out that it is the very power of music to mobilize people that makes it a tool to be feared by restrictive regimes (Street 2003, p. 117). The qualities of music that grant it this utility/power are its accessibility, communal aspects (often it is performed in groups and people work together toward a common aim) (May 2013), and the way it can tap into memory and emotions (May 2013; Elias et al. 2011; Tacchi 1998). It is these conditions that can both mobilize people to act politically or to feel a sense of belonging to a group, with or without political aims.

While much of the literature from cultural studies, sociology, and anthropology that investigates the role of art as a tool for belonging or political expression is focused on music, we argue that many of the assertions about music in this area can be applied to numerous collective art forms. Various collective art forms share the same qualities as those mentioned above with regard to music. This is not to say that music does not have unique qualities, but in the cases explored here we find that various art forms can foster political action and belonging.

Undoubtedly, the arts, in their accessibility, make certain types of political expression possible for disadvantaged groups who have fewer opportunities to take political action—in this case, asylum seekers and refugees (Martiniello and Lafleur 2008, p. 1207)—, but the arts are also a pathway to other types of less visible belonging. As Baily and Collyer state, "the circumstances of migration are likely to have a profound effect on how music fits into the migrant experience" (Baily and Collyer 2006, p. 172). The arts can have different meanings and impacts on a person's life depending on how they have migrated and what their aims are in their new place of residence. Often times, the chances to blend in through participation in arts groups are not as numerous as the opportunities to speak out. However, it is the interpretation of arts practices as either political or not that may impact the artists' desires to be seen and heard or to remain an inconspicuous part of a group. Martiniello and Lafleur (2010, p. 214) state, " ... the specialists of Cultural Studies tend to exaggerate the political dimension of art and culture in general. For many of them, nothing can be without political relevance". Rose, on the other hand, cautions against overlooking the political relevance of artistic production that does not have an explicit political message. She urges audiences to consider the many facets of the various contexts surrounding the production of the art.

> Rap in its infancy was considered to be 'party music' with no political significance or aim, but as it evolved it took forms that were explicitly/obviously political. [...] to dismiss rappers who do not choose so-called 'political' subjects as 'having no politically resistive meaning' requires ignoring the complex web of institutional policing to which all rappers are subject. (Rose 1991, p. 276)

What matters in the determination of which is art is political, and indeed its meaning overall, is the intention of the artist, the reception of the audience, the sociocultural and historical context, and a host of other factors (Roy 2010; Becker 1982). This often makes it difficult to determine how/whether art is political.

2. Methodology

We gathered the material presented in this article mainly through participant observation. Emerson et al. describe participant observation as "establishing a place in some natural setting on a relatively long-term basis in order to investigate, experience and represent the social life and social processes that occur in that setting ... " (Emerson et al. 2001, p. 353). This research method, for which we took an anthropological approach, enabled us to comply with the ethical concerns encountered when studying issues related to vulnerable populations (Harrell-Bond 1986). In fact, it is often the case that interrogating individuals who have undergone[1] an interview process that led to legitimating or, conversely, de-legitimating their presence in Belgium, through granting or denying a regular legal status, was often inappropriate. In situations where this was not the case and it was deemed that due to their regularized situation or their keen interest in being interviewed, interlocutors were interviewed in order to supplement the material gathered from participation[2]. Collaboration[3] in the artistic practices of interlocutors produced knowledge in a process that allowed for a more sensuous understanding where it was crucial to share life experiences in a mutual exchange between the researchers and their research participants. All participants, including the researchers, were thus equal parts of a creative process that combined each one's thoughts and narratives. In this type of collaboration, artistic products are not ready-made objects of analysis, but rather the results of a shared process that involves the research participants and the researcher himself/herself in this production of knowledge (O'Neill 2008). May (2013) explains that "cultural belongings are experienced in an embodied manner, for example when singing a national anthem, wearing a familiar piece of clothing or eating a national dish" (p. 131) and Pink (2009) advises researchers to have experiences that are as similar as possible to those of one's participants. The researchers personally engaged in the artistic work of the participants in order to get a better/different understanding of their sense of belonging. This level of collaboration allowed the researchers to uncover the differing aims and motivations of the interlocutors through the process of creating an artistic product.

Concerning the artistic practices of undocumented migrants in Liege that are analyzed in the next section, they have been observed within the framework of a research project focused on public opinion on migrants (already mentioned above, see footnote 4) which also included the study of the mobilization activities of migrants themselves. To implement this study, the researcher participated in several artistic workshops, and in particular in the writing workshops that led to several theatre representations and exhibitions, as well as in a theatre workshop held at the Theatre of Liege. As we will see in detail below, the analysis of the collected—and co-produced—material shows how the arts have potential effects on the local population. The research conducted in Brussels was part of a PhD project in which the researcher endeavored to understand young migrants' homemaking strategies and sense of belonging in the city. The research was carried out by attending rehearsals, singing and playing drums with the group, and performing at various events. In the instances when the researcher was not participating in arts practices, the researcher was participating in demonstrations and manifestations that were a part of the wider research aim.

---

[1] Or that are still undergoing, as far as asylum seekers are concerned.
[2] Informed consent was always obtained prior to interviews and questions concerning participants' past were not asked in order to avoid re-traumatization.
[3] In fact, some members of the group also participated in preparing the researcher's intervention in an artistic and scientific event by recording and editing a video showing some of their artistic workshops. See https://traverses.hypotheses.org/ (accessed on 17 January 2019), communication by Bertholet et al. (2018).

3. Arts to Be Visible

3.1. Liege, A "Welcoming City"

Former capital of an ecclesiastic principality and trigger site of successive democratic revolutions, the thousand-year-old city of Liege was characterized by an economic growth in the 19th century due to the expansion of the coal industry and the development of armory and glass working[4]. This fact, together with a process of progressive urbanization and development of modern infrastructures, attracted a labor workforce from abroad. After the recession that came when the coal mines were forced to close starting from the 1950s, new sectors of economy and services developed. The province of Liege counts 1,105,733 inhabitants, and the city 196,685 on the 1st January, 2019[5]. In the last available analysis of the composition of the population realized by the municipality in 2015, 37,377 inhabitants were registered with foreign nationality—25.5% of that year's population[6]. While some scholars define Liege as a "post-migration city" (Martiniello 2011) due to its migration history, others also underline that this make-up is still continuously re-defined by human mobility (Bousetta et al. 2018, pp. 71–72). As a consequence, space for migrants and cultural diversity is still the object of debates (Bousetta et al. 2018, p. 72) that intersect the local environment and the state context. The enduring restriction of migration policies, also resulting in a process of the securitization of migration that includes repeated state actions against irregular migrants (such as raids, imprisonments and evictions), puts constraints on the local governance of migration issues. On the one hand, this process has resulted in an increase in the number of undocumented migrants since the last regularization program held in 2009 (Bousetta et al. 2018, p. 81) and, on the other hand, it undermines the possibilities of challenging this situation. Within this overall context, where public opinion and related actions are polarized—in the sense that people deal with migration issues either through civic engagement to support them, or through overt opposition[7]—the city of Liege, with its main institutional, political, social and cultural actors still tries to position itself as relatively open to migrants. Recently labeled as a "welcoming city" (ville hospitalière), following a citizens' campaign supported by a Belgian NGO[8], Liege engaged in adapting its actions and services to the needs and claims of migrants living in its territory. This approach is also supposed to concern undocumented migrants, and this means that, officially, the local government promotes a general climate of "tolerance" in addition to guaranteeing certain rights[9].

3.2. La Voix des Sans-Papiers de Liège

The history of the occupation of public buildings (or churches) by undocumented migrants in the city of Liege—and thus of these individuals' presence in the city—goes back at least to the years that preceded two main regularization programs, which occurred in 1999 and 2009. As far as the collective "*La Voix des Sans-Papiers de Liège*" (VSP from now on) is concerned, it was created in 2015 and grew from the occupation of an uninhabited public building. The building was occupied by a small group of sub-Saharan migrants whose irregular situation was the result of the rejection of their asylum demand in Belgium or the expiration of their visa (for tourism or education). At first, the needs of the collective consisted of securing accommodation for people—women, men and children of all ages—who were

---

[4] See the municipality official website at: https://www.liege.be/en/discover/tourism/discover-liege/history-of-liege (accessed on 16 March 2019).
[5] See the Belgian government official statistics available at https://www.ibz.rrn.fgov.be/fileadmin/user_upload/fr/pop/statistiques/population-bevolking-20190101.pdf (accessed on 16 March 2019).
[6] See https://www.liege.be/fr/vie-communale/administration/liege-en-chiffres/tableaux-de-bord-population/tableau-de-bord-population-2015.pdf (accessed on 16 March 2019).
[7] Such process is the object of a recent research project funded by the Belgian Federal Science Policy Office (BELSPO) and aimed at studying the "Public opinion, mobilisations and policies concerning asylum seekers and refugees in anti-immigrants times (Europe and Belgium)" (PUMOMIG). The ethnographic material presented in this paper and concerning migrants' action in the city of Liege has been collected within the framework of this project.
[8] See the website of the campaign at https://www.communehospitaliere.be/ (accessed on 17 January 2019).
[9] Among them are the rights of "urgent medical care" (*aide médicale urgente*) and education.

living on the streets. The following quote by one of the founders of the initiative, now residing legally in Belgium after his regularization through family reunification, narrates the beginning of the initiative and its initial aims:

> "*Sans-papiers* were around ten […] we occupied the building, it is there [in Sclessin, a neighbourhood of Liege] that the occupation started […]. During the first days the *soutiens*[10] managed to bring food, volunteers connected the water, they set electricity on, they took boilers, they did all that was needed to occupy the building".
>
> (Salim, recorded on 30 January 2018)[11]

In time, the group grew in number and it moved to another public building which used to be a local school (see Figure 1). This movement, that geographically brought the collective closer to the city centre, also corresponded to a political change. In fact, from this moment on, the interactions with public authorities and the civil society intensified and also led to some economic support (beside the fact that the occupation was locally accepted[12]. It was then possible to set other priorities and push the aims of the collective forward:

> "After a month […] because if we want to create an effective [social] movement we have to organize meetings, […] we made the meetings of the collective. […] we were united for a cause. […] [so that] the sans-papiers as such could assume their status and claim it high and loud and say: 'I am a *sans-papiers*', because it is not a crime. […] people hide themselves because they are *sans-papiers*. […] but it's the system that makes you a *sans-papiers*, and if you really want to fight against this, you have first to start diagnosing [*diagnostiquer* in French] yourself". (Salim, recorded on 30 January 2018)

These words are similar to De Genova (2002) theory about the legal production of illegality, and how people begin to claim their rights by re-appropriating "illegal status". Such rights consist of the authorization to live in Belgium and access to the civic liberties that are associated with this.

Figure 1. The buildings inhabited by the members of the collective © La Voix des Sans-Papiers de Liège, Facebook page.

---

[10] Literally meaning "supports", this term is used by the members of the VSP to name those Belgian citizens who mobilize to help with the actions implemented by the VSP and that gather in what is called the "support committee". This group also mediate with institutional and other local actors when direct interlocution with undocumented migrants is precluded for several—logistic, strategic or constraining—reasons.
[11] All names used for research participants are aliases.
[12] However, the city later sold the buildings to a private owner. The occupants were not evicted, but relocation is needed urgently and is being negotiated as we write this article.

3.3. Claiming Existence

The rights claiming process of the VSP (addressing human and civic rights, beside—and together with—regularization) is developed through concrete actions that testify to migrants' active role in the socio-cultural local life of the city. These actions consist of—among other things—working, attending school/classes (for children and adults), participating in creative workshops, protests and artistic productions. For their implementation, migrants can rely on the support of a network of actors including associations and NGOs working on migration issues, cultural associations, local services and institutions, political representatives, and individual mobilized citizens. The analysis of the actions of socio-cultural participation implemented by undocumented migrants leads to the emergence of a series of topics of which two are particularly relevant to the issues raised by this article. First, these activities are the locations where the performance of agency occurs despite structural constraints that individuals face due to their (il)legal statuses. The actions taken by migrants improve their daily lives and are a means of performing their struggle against the contemporary migration policies. However, we may question whether the spaces (and in particular the cultural spaces) in which migrants exert these actions are concrete locations for resistance or remain marginalized sites where migrants are again kept apart and whose exclusion is thus perpetuated with the alleged complicity of humanitarian aid. bell hooks proposes to solve this dilemma, to some extent, by making "a definite distinction between that marginality which is imposed by oppressive structures and that marginality one chooses as a site of resistance—as location of radical openness and possibility" (Hooks 1990, p. 153). Sociological marginality is transformed into rhetorical marginality (Gilbert 2004, p. 5), and this process enables us to put forward the subversive nature of migrants' actions (and in particular, as we will see below, of theatre practice). We assume, together with our research participants, that these actions convey a representation of undocumented migrants as active and autonomous subjects claiming their right to exist on Belgian soil:

> "I was so upset when they said: 'oh poor people, poor people', it's always us the 'poor people'. When we are in need, we can ask for some help ... for me, help is necessary, but help must lead to freedom. Help cannot be permanent, help can lead to do without help. [...] they want us to be dependent. [...] actually, the fight of the *sans-papiers* has been taken in pincers [*prise en tenaille*, in French]". (Salim, recorded 30 January 2018)

We underline the importance of examining "to what extent arts are used and could be a useful tool in local incorporation" (Martiniello 2015, p. 1232), that is to "address the issue of incorporation of migrants from an uncommon perspective that also informs the process by which newcomers become—or do not—full members of a given society" (Martiniello 2015, p. 1233). In this case, arts constitute the basis of political action. It is through art practices that collective identities are positioned against the "local social and political order", thus playing a crucial role in social and political mobilization (Martiniello and Lafleur 2008; Mattern 1998)" (Martiniello 2015, p. 1233).

For the members of the VSP, arts are crucial to participation in the local socio-cultural life of the city and to their ability to claim civic rights. One of our research participants, a Belgian artist and worker within the domain of education, said: "with an artistic and cultural action they produce something that carries a meaning, that will resonate within a public" (Paul, recorded on 30 November 2017). Indeed, "artistic expressions can help build bridges to facilitate encounters (Vertovec 2007) between populations with different ethnic origins sharing the same city or the same neighbourhood" (Martiniello 2015, p. 1232), and this creates spaces for raising voices. The artistic activities of the VSP involved professional and non-professional artists, migrants and non-migrants, and these activities are considered art items because they were the result of a process of creation (Gell 1998). A series of writing, painting and theatre workshops were the origin of these art products. These workshops were locations for sharing experiences, expertise, thoughts, etc., among people with different stories and profiles, and where people could create art items to communicate these shared contents to those outside of the group. Among these art products were audio-visual creations shown within the framework of a local artistic event. During this festival, the owners of the villas in a middle-class neighborhood of the city of Liege opened the doors of their houses to artists (usually painters) who could then show and sell their works[13]. The members of the VSP, due to the intervention of a local resident, were able to use an uninhabited villa, owned by an institutional foundation, as the setting for their artistic productions. The first of these, located in the secondary entrance of the villa, was the installation of an audio-tape where one can listen to the life experiences of some members of the VSP (Figure 2).

Figure 2. Installation at the Parcours d'artistes de Cointe, Liege, 20 May 2018 © Elsa Mescoli.

Here is an excerpt of one woman's recording:

"I want to add something, some memories about Belgium, when I came, I was relieved, I thought I had found ... [...] where I had my rights, my freedom. But I was wrong, [...] after the negative answer [about refugee status request] I found myself as someone who has no right, no freedom, but I learnt with my family that you need to fight to go forward, I always fight to go forward, and I still have good memories. When I will have my rights, my freedom of saying what I think, my freedom of doing what I want, [...] I always fight to have this. With the problems of not having documents, we learn how to help each other, [...] we always have the hope ... ". (Fieldnotes, 20 May 2018)

Through narrating her migration experience, this woman describes the deception of the expectations that she had before leaving her country of origin as well as the motivations that push her to fight for her rights—the civic rights connected with receiving a residence permit through regularization.

---

[13] *Le parcours d'artistes à Cointe.*

Another room of the villa became the setting for representing thoughts on "vital space". Images of people lying on the floor showed how many persons could sleep (and live) in that uninhabited room. A text accompanied the installation:

"Life becomes for oneself as a globe that turns around itself. In this world, everyone must live without obstructing the life of the others. In this world, there are so many people that live in an incredible precariousness, and all this is caused by the others' wickedness. In this world, and more precisely in Belgium, there exist people, migrants, men, women, children, in illegal situation, called *sans-papiers*, that struggle to find a vital space". (Idem.)

In the garden, a tree was decorated with some "questions without answers" (Figure 3a), such as:

"Why so little sharing of our richness? Why so little welcome to men and women that escape from their countries because they are hungry, because they are persecuted? Why Belgium does not give papers? Why isn't there free circulation of people? Why seven years in Belgium without documents? Why I miss my family? Why and how will we put things in order in this unfair world? How can we live together? To whom asking help? To what all this is useful? How to get out of this suffering? Where do we go after this long struggle? When and how the end will come?". (Idem.)

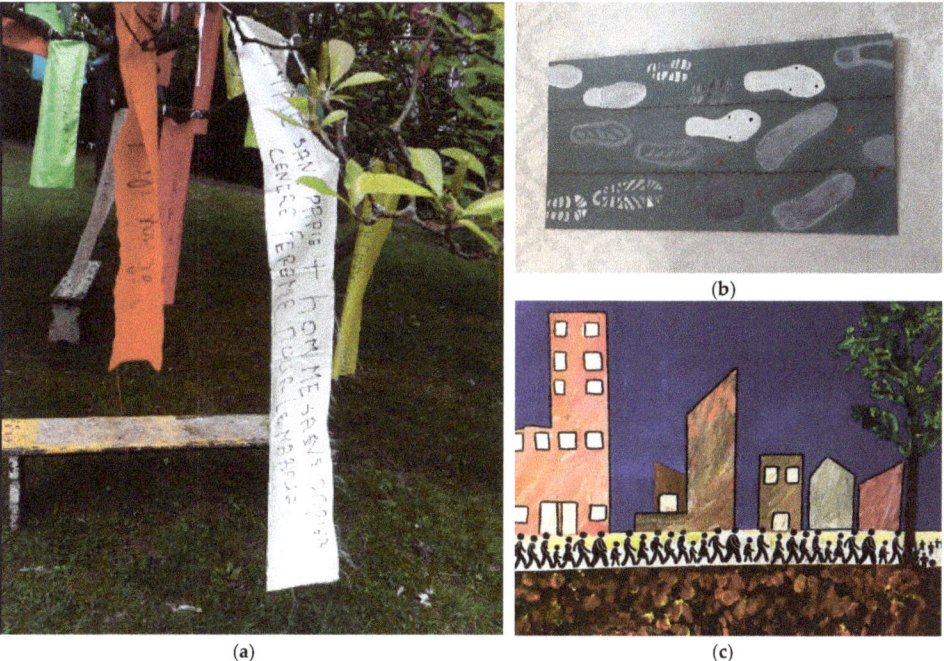

Figure 3. The tree of the "questions without answers" (**a**) and some paintings of the collective (**b**,**c**), Parcours d'artistes de Cointe, 20 May 2018 © Elsa Mescoli and La Voix des Sans-Papiers de Liège, used with permission.

Some paintings depicted "the path of a migrant: the departure, the ghosts, the hopes; the journey, the path of difficulties; distance, absence, roots, wandering" (idem, Figure 3b,c).

Some members of the VSP also participated in a project that the Theatre of Liege implemented with the aim of fighting discrimination through arts. Some theatre workshops trained the bodies and the gazes of the participants (here, undocumented migrants, actors, and local students) to move within a shared space and to coordinate movements with others by interacting with them visually and bodily. After this exercise, the focus was on the practice of the clown, an artistic way to become other than oneself and to experience alterity (or one's own experience through the gaze of a dissociated-self)[14]. We can read in this excerpt of a dialogue between the professional actor leading the workshop and one of the participants on how this artistic performance conveyed meaning related to being *sans-papiers*:

- Do you have something to say?
- I am tired.
- Why are you tired Toni?
- I am illegal in Belgium.
- Explain me.
- I am a sans-papiers.
- OK, so this [the nose] is the symbol of sans-papiers? (Fieldnotes, 30 March 2018).

During this and several other similar moments of performance, the effects of illegality on everyday life were brought to the scene. In fact, an intrinsic relationship connects theatre with reality (Beeman 1993, p. 372, referring to Schechner 1985). However, the context of the performances is governed by rules that are different from those governing everyday actions. Rituals to become other than himself/herself accompany the practice of the clown. Before starting the performance, the actor needs to embody his or her character with a series of actions focused on the body:

"Breathe deeply from your nose, close your eyes, and as a puppet, we cut the threads [the actor sitting on a chair leaves his/her arms and bust fall to the floor]. When you are completely relaxed, you wear the nose [...]. You lift your head with your eyes closed, and when you open your eyes, everything will be possible, except what is normal". (Fieldnotes, 26 April 2018)[15]

Once on the stage, the new character (the clown) can reverse hierarchies and power dynamics through capitalizing on difference and stigma as evidence of existence. As Goffman puts it, the humor of the stigmatized makes him a "half-hero" who "is made to guilelessly outwit a normal of imposing status" (Goffman 2009, p. 108). Some individuals, who are legally excluded from the society, create places where they can perform their life and find their voice through artistic performance. Through humor in particular, the artist can express a social critique (Gilbert 2004), thus re-positioning her or himself as an active actor in the society. From this position, undocumented migrants re-acquire a degree of freedom in a social space where the borders of social categories fade. The performance of subordination and marginalization gives visibility to these processes and to the status that derives from them.

On other occasions, however, the topics connected with the issue of illegality were not directly mentioned and it seemed that the aesthetic scope of the activity prevailed. In fact, art performance was also an end in itself. It offered possibilities to engage in a cultural activity, to spend time with people, and to find some way to belong.

The audiences of these artistic projects were different in the two examples mentioned above. In the first case, the described festival is an open event attended by any individual who may be generally interested in arts and not necessarily in migration issues. People visiting the villas because of their artistic interests almost casually came across the artistic products realized by the VSP and thus the contents that these products conveyed—notably, of claiming regularization and the civic rights that derive from it. Unexpected discussions on these topics emerged among unaware observers. Concerning the theatre workshop, the first meetings that are described here did not yet imply the

---

[14] On the role of theatre and humor for marginalized categories of people (including a gender approach), see Gilbert (2004).
[15] These words are from the professional actor guiding the theatre workshops.

participation of the public since they were more like training sessions. However, some spectators were almost always present and they included, besides the researcher who observed the workshop, members of the theatre and other people who supported the activities of the VSP. The variation of the public in terms of its composition and scope did not necessarily impact the effect of the performances. In fact, in all the described cases, the performances reached an audience and in doing so, they triggered discussion on migration issues and they brought migrants into visible action. The artistic activities of the VSP are renowned locally as well as beyond the territory of Liege, since at least two of the theatre plays that they created are regularly performed in different locations in Belgium. The political scope of these artistic initiatives is evident: these actions are intentionally aimed at giving visibility to undocumented migrants and stating the need of regularization procedures that would enable the recognition of their legitimate and legal existence in the country.

4. Arts to Be Invisible

4.1. Superdiverse Brussels

Clear in the above examples is that art is regularly and effectively used as a form of protest, a way of highlighting issues, calling for change, and sharing one's own unique position and struggles with a wider audience. Some artists, however, want to simply be labeled as artists and do 'art for the sake of art' or indeed participate in the arts to build community and find a sense of 'belonging'. Brussels, unarguably a superdiverse (Vertovec 2007) city with a long immigration history and a prominent place on the international political stage, is a place where one can choose to be highly visible or almost entirely invisible. Brussels as a city has some unique characteristics that set it apart from other major metropoles/global cities. As of 1 January 2018, the population of the Brussels Capital Region was 1,198,726. The number of people with nationalities from the 28 European Union member states (and not also having Belgian nationality) was 276,098 and third-country nationals was 141,009[16]. In 2015, the immigrant and foreign-born population accounted for 62% of the total population of the city, coming in second to Dubai which, at 83%, had the highest percentage of immigrant foreign-born population in a city (International Organization for Migration 2015). In addition to hosting numerous European and international institutions and the workforce that comes with them, Belgium also receives a significant number of refugees and asylum seekers. Their situation in Brussels has sometimes garnered international attention, with, at various times, hundreds of asylum seekers queuing outside the Foreigners Office and sleeping in the park across the street. When hundreds of rejected Afghan asylum seekers sought asylum in a Brussels church, it remained a regular story in local and international news for several months (Willner-Reid 2015). Brussels, under the spotlight brought by international and EU institutions, has the same struggles as many other cities when it comes to the politics of accepting refugees and granting asylum and how people are cared for while their situations are unsettled. Against this backdrop, Brussels fancies itself an artistic city, having attracted a large number of artists despite the competition of larger cities with thriving art communities, such as Paris, nearby. Brussels has a large number of exhibits and artistic initiatives, often with the focus of depicting the city and local interpretations of the urban environment (Reverseau 2019). These depictions and reimaginings are created by anyone having ties to the city and national belongings rarely factor in, and, as Costanzo and Zibouh state, arts can create a space for "a certain affirmation of an identity that, in this case, transcends prescribed ethnic and migrant identities and attempts to establish a new means of self-assertion in the post-migration context by promoting a place-based (Bruxellois) identity" (Costanzo and Zibouh 2014, p. 56).

---

[16] https://statbel.fgov.be/en/themes/population/structure-population#panel-12.

4.2. Music Groups as Sanctuaries: The Case of Undocumented Migrants in a Brussels Church

In Brussels, there are numerous organizations and groups rallying for the rights of undocumented migrants either as their main mission or in addition to other activities. In 2013, a group of hundreds of rejected asylum seekers from Afghanistan were offered sanctuary in a Brussels church. Initially, this event was widely covered in the media and there were regular protests that garnered significant community support. According to Eurostat, more than 20,000 Afghans sought asylum in the European Union in 2013, and approximately 1300 applied in Belgium (Bitoulas 2014). Public outcry was partially to thank for the subsequent actions of the office of Maggie De Block, who in 2014 was the Minister of Justice charged with Asylum, Immigration, Social Integration, and Poverty Reduction in the Di Rupo Government. Her office asked the failed asylum seekers to reapply for asylum. The majority of the group from the church decided to go ahead with these procedures which meant that they were allowed to live in the centers that are provided for asylum seekers while they awaited the outcome of their applications. As a result, most of the Afghans left the church by February 2014 (Willner-Reid 2015, p. 514). The Afghans who remained in the church in January to June 2015, when fieldwork was conducted, were mostly single men in their 20s and 30s—those who felt that they would have their applications for asylum rejected upon resubmission and thus be deported.

The church remained open at this time and served as the 'Afghan info point' where anyone could walk in during the day and read posters created by the undocumented residents to learn about their situation (Figure 4). In fact, it was also possible to simply walk up to the residents and inquire about their situation. Even though media attention had abated, the situation of the Afghans in the church still enjoyed great local notoriety. They were still incredibly 'visible' even if it seemed that the city was no longer paying attention to their plight. One former resident of the church, Amir, stopped living there when he was offered a room in a friend's house. Life in the church clearly revolved around the regular protest marches and political actions of the group (Figure 5). He said he came back to the church often to visit his friends, but he appreciated being able to focus on other parts of his life.

Figure 4. Inside the church. 15 January 2015 © Shannon Damery.

Figure 5. Police and 'sans papiers security' at a manifestation in Brussels. 4 March 2015 © Shannon Damery.

He decided to dedicate some of his time to a music group of undocumented people, but this was not his first choice. There are places in Brussels specifically for immigrant artists to practice their work, one of which will be described in greater detail in the following example, but Amir wanted to join a music group in The Centre for Fine Arts in Brussels (BOZAR). He found this was impossible without being able to show some kind of identification. As Martiniello (2015) stresses, arts can be a vehicle for gaining attention for a platform, and it can also be a tool for incorporation and building bridges between cultures. Sometimes, however, as was the case with Amir, these are two separate aims. Amir wished, at least in the artistic part of his life, to be connected with Belgian society but not necessarily to be part of a highly visible platform for a political aim.

In her study, Rotas (2012) explains how refugees helped to change the category of British art and what it means to be British. She gives an account of refugee artists whose work was displayed in an exhibition of British art. While Rotas tells us that the cultural grounding of the artwork is still very clear, and the audience is aware that the works represent cultural experiences they have not encountered or do not understand, cultural transmission is still occurring and the host culture is being influenced (Rotas 2012, p. 212). Rotas further explains that the definition of the refugee's work as 'British' contributes to the remaking of "place Britain" and the idea of Britishness (Rotas 2012, p. 219). If these works had been displayed in an exhibition of immigrant art, for example, the work would have been cast in a different light and the audience invited to focus on *differences*. As it stands, the refugees gained unofficial status as 'British' in a significant type of acceptance into the community. It is important to note that these groups, as useful and well-intentioned as they are, may still serve to separate migrants from the wider society. Amir ultimately joined a group of undocumented musicians where the teacher did not ask for identification. He seemed to appreciate this group and find through it some type of belonging, in the way described by May (2013). Amir said that the people in the group were all from different countries and that their singing together was "like a solidarity action" (interview, 16 February 2015). This is similar to May's explanation that, "music can also form part of collective experience and identity, as evidence whenever Liverpool Football Club fans sing 'You'll never walk alone'" (May 2013, p. 135). This action and group, however, still did not have the aim of promoting a common political cause of the participants and making their particular situation more visible. Roy and Dowd explain that groups "use music as a tool for building identity—an 'us' (Roy 2002) The relationship between a group and music flows two ways: Music is identified by people inside (and out-side) the group as belonging to it, and membership in the group is marked partly by embracing this music" (Roy and Dowd 2010, p. 190). In many cases, it seems that people wish to somehow 'disappear into belonging' and become less visible by being part of a group with less politically or cause driven aims.

4.3. Belonging without Politics? The Case of the Roma Music Group

Another example of this phenomenon was a music group based in a cultural centre in Brussels. The aim of the group itself was to make visible a group of people and a political aim. The centre was a non-profit funded in part by Flemish cultural initiatives. It provided a place and materials for refugees and asylum-seeking artists to practice their art. In addition to supporting these artists, the organization also spoke about encouraging discussion around social issues since the international make-up of Brussels makes it ripe for such dialogue. As part of a collaborative effort with other organizations, the centre created a musical group that for the purposes of this article will be called The Balkan Review. The specific aims of the review were to promote the inclusion and positive image of the Roma community in Europe, and may be linked to an increased interest from EU bodies to promote Roma inclusion across EU member states. The review made certain to include Roma and non-Roma musicians and directors and seemed to pride itself on the fact that it was initiated by a Roma organization.

The project is still ongoing, and the website described the aims of the project in the following way:

> With this project, [org. name] aims to generate more insight and understanding for the large Roma immigration from the Balkans to more economically successful countries like the Netherlands, Belgium and Germany. Only when you know why they came here and what the position of the Roma in their home countries is, can you properly understand the immigration of Roma. (...) The fact that this project is also supported and initiated by the Roma community, which heretofore was seen as a closed off community, makes this project remarkable.

Because members were often coming and going, it is impossible to say exactly how many members of the Brussels Balkan Review there actually were and from which backgrounds, but in addition to Roma members, there were people from many immigrant, non-immigrant, European and non-European backgrounds.

The organizers and funders of the group had more specific aims and stronger opinions than the performers on the identities they were promoting, what kind of 'integration' they wanted to foster, and the audience they wanted to reach. They were hoping to promote the inclusion of Roma youth in Belgium seemingly by reaching a non-Roma audience of 'locals'. The venues included schools, cultural organizations, and a large concert hall in Antwerp. The performers and director, however, cared about the music they were producing above all else. All of the young people said that they came because they liked the group and had fun, and because their friends came. One participant from the Balkan region said that he came because he liked playing music he used to play with his family. Another participant, who was undocumented, joined the group simply to be with his friends and learn other languages. He said that he was involved in a lot of political actions but the music group was just for fun (fieldnotes, 22 March 2015). As stated above, the arts are connected to feelings of nostalgia, but Baily suggests that music may also offer a feeling of security.

> ... the primary effect of music is to give the listener a feeling of security, for it symbolizes the place where he was born, his earliest childhood satisfactions, his religious experience, his pleasure in community doings, his courtship and his work—any or all of these personality-shaping experiences. (Baily 1999, p. 11)

In both the rehearsing and performing, it seemed that the participants felt a sense of security in their belonging to the group. Even for the researcher, who was not familiar with the songs and types of music the group performed, the practice of performing together in the group brought back memories of performing in choirs in the past. There was also no concern from the undocumented members of the group that the audiences might not be receptive or that there would be a lack of acceptance. The audiences who attended the concerts did appear to be quite mixed with many different languages being spoken, but a large portion of each audience were the friends and family of the performers, so it remains unclear if the organization reached its intended audience. In any case, the performances were always met with enthusiasm from the audience—the bigger concerts seeing people getting up and dancing to the music, some who knew the 'traditional dances' and some who clearly did not.

The group could be divided along several different lines, and one of these was between members from the Balkans and those who were not. While this division, and others, were important, it was also important that there was group cohesion built around the performing of these songs and in everyone becoming familiar with and appreciating the music. Having a good performance took precedence over the aim of promoting Roma culture, which was still a result of project, but not the main aim of the participants. Martiniello (2018) noted the emergence of post-racial groups among young artists in Belgium stating that young people growing up in multi-cultural, diverse environments see this as a simple fact of life and when engaging in artistic practices; the outcome of the art project is the main focus.

> "I call this urban generation post-racial not because they have become colour-blind but because the traditional forms of categorization (racial, ethnic, gender, class, etc.) seem to lose salience in their daily peer group inter- actions. Their ethnic and racial identification do not orient the forms of inter-action and cooperation they develop with other urban youngsters. The shared artistic project is much more important than their alleged ethnic or racial identity".
> (Martiniello 2018, p. 1153)

This idea is significant when looking at immigrant artists who do not wish to be seen as 'other', and wish to 'disappear' into a group where their belonging is not questioned and they do not have to be part of a particular political aim.

5. Concluding Remarks

These examples enable us to state that, in spite of structural constraints, art is a means (and a product) through which migrants, independent from their legal status, participate in the local socio-cultural life and elaborate concrete claims concerning their own situation as well as global concerns that are related to it—such as migration governance and politics. Art practice constitutes a creative political engagement in the local context (Salzbrunn 2014) and also a way for people to find belonging without caveats (Martiniello 2018). In Belgium, the contemporary climate on migration reflects the debates spreading at the European level. The situation is particularly difficult due to the restrictive policies and practices adopted by the former right-wing Secretary of State in charge of these affairs at the federal level[17]. The local environments (cities) can constitute spaces of resistance to the overall politics, in which migrants who are made invisible by the rejection of their demands for regularization and the denial of their existence on Belgian soil, become visible through concrete actions. Legitimating their presence and action in the public space in spite of their legal status permits the blurring of the boundaries between illegality and legality. Culture and artistic practices in post-migration urban settings emerge here as tools to promote social cohesion and integration through the action of formal and informal networks (Clavier and Kauppinen 2014; Vanderwaeren 2014) involving a variety of social profiles of which migrants—and in our case, undocumented migrants in particular—are a part.

---

[17] Theo Francken, Nieuw-Vlaamse Alliantie (N-VA). No relevant changes, as far as the approach to migration issues is concerned, occurred in spite of his recent resignation and his replacement by Maggie De Block, Open VLD, already mentioned above in this article.

Participation in arts practices can result in the blurring of divisions between people of different backgrounds and migratory statuses. This is precisely what makes the arts a way for migrants to become 'invisible' by finding unofficial acceptance in a host society. Indeed, we saw how art practice is not only a means, but also an end in itself. It constitutes an aesthetic and corporeal device that undocumented migrants can, and do, experience in positive terms. Art is a vehicle through which our participants activated their agency in order to claim belonging in Belgium despite their status as undocumented or 'other', by making themselves and their situation more visible or by choosing to, at least temporarily, leave their classification of being 'other' behind and merging seamlessly into an arts group. While the intention of the artists here is key, this is often a difficult aspect to unravel and fully understand. Long-term engagement in arts projects through participant observation allowed us to better understand this dimension, but there are still subtleties that were perhaps less apparent and intention is incredibly nuanced. Research in this domain undoubtedly profits from employing participatory and co-creation methods, and future research would benefit from a better understanding of the impact of audience reactions to artists' endeavors to find belonging, either through increased or decreased visibility.

Author Contributions: E.M. wrote the sections concerning the artistic practices developed by migrants in the city of Liege, while S.D. wrote the sections concerning the artistic practices developed by migrants in the city of Brussels. Both authors wrote all the other sections (Introduction, Methodology, Concluding Remarks).

Funding: Belgian Federal Science Policy Office (BELSPO), funding agency of the project "Public opinion, mobilisations and policies concerning asylum seekers and refugees in anti-immigrant times (Europe and Belgium)" (PUMOMIG). Elsa Mescoli collected the ethnographic material presented in this paper and concerning migrants' action in the city of Liege within the framework of this project. The researched conducted by Shannon Damery received funding from the European Union's Seventh Framework Programme (FP7/2007-2013) under grant agreement n° 316796. She gathered the materials in this article thanks to funding as a fellow in the Marie Curie Initial Training Network.

Acknowledgments: We thank all the artists mentioned directly or indirectly in this article that let us explore and participate in their art practice, and all other migrants that were involved in the research connected with the material presented here.

Conflicts of Interest: The authors declare no conflict of interest.

References

Baily, John. 1999. Music and refugee lives: Afghans in Eastern Iran and California. *Forced Migration Review* 6: 10–12.

Baily, John, and Michael Collyer. 2006. Introduction: Music and migration. *Journal of Ethnic and Migration Studies* 32: 167–82. [CrossRef]

Becker, Howard. 1982. *Art Worlds*. Berkeley: University of California Press.

Beeman, William O. 1993. The anthropology of theater and spectacle. *Annual Review of Anthropology* 22: 369–93. [CrossRef]

Bertholet, Edith Dieng, Honoré Abdourahmane Ndayishimiye, and Elsa Mescoli. 2018. La création dans l'inconfort: L'expérience théâtrale pour et par les migrants sans-papiers de Liège. Paper and video presented at the Conference: Migrations: nos voix, nos chemins de traverse rencontre entre arts, sciences et militances, Marseille, France, October 25.

Bitoulas, Alexandros. 2014. Eurostat Data in Focus: Population and Social Conditions (Published online March 2014). Available online: http://ec.europa.eu/eurostat/documents/4168041/5948933/KS-QA-14-003-EN.PDF/3309ae42-431c-42d7-99a3-534ed5b93294 (accessed on 1 December 2017).

Bousetta, Hassan, Lafleur Jean-Michel, and Gregor Stangherlin. 2018. Ville multi-inter-culturelle? Discours, pratiques, réalités. In *Regards sur la ville. Echanges et réflexions à partir de Liège*. Edited by Brahy Rachel, Dumont Elisabeth, Fontaine Pierre and Christine Ruelle. Liège: Presses Universitaires de Liège, pp. 69–89.

Clavier, Berndt, and Asko Kauppinen. 2014. Art for integration: Political rationalities and technologies of governmentalisation in the city of Malmö. *Identities* 21: 10–25. [CrossRef]

Costanzo, Joseph, and Fatima Zibouh. 2014. Mobilisation strategies of individual and institutional actors in Brussels' artistic and cultural scenes. *Identities* 21: 42–59. [CrossRef]

De Genova, Nicholas P. 2002. Migrant "illegality" and deportability in everyday life. *Annual Review of Anthropology* 31: 419–47. [CrossRef]

DiMaggio, Paul, and Patricia Fernández-Kelly. 2015. Immigration and the arts: A theoretical inquiry. *Ethnic and Racial Studies* 38: 1236–44. [CrossRef]

Elias, Nelly, Lemish Dafna, and Natalia Khvorostianov. 2011. Britney Spears Remained in Russia: Dynamics of Musical Preferences in the Integration of Immigrant Adolescents. *Journal of Ethnic and Migration Studies* 37: 61–77. [CrossRef]

Emerson, Robert, Fretz Rachel, and Linda Shaw. 2001. Participant Observation and Fieldnotes. In *Handbook of Ethnography*. Edited by Paul Atkinson, Amanda Coffey, Sara Delamont, John Lofland and Lyn Lofland. London: Sage Publications Ltd., pp. 352–68.

Gell, Alfred. 1998. *Art and Agency: An Anthropological Theory*. Oxford: Clarendon Press.

Gilbert, Joanne R. 2004. *Performing Marginality: Humor, Gender, and Cultural Critique*. Detroit: Wayne State University Press.

Goffman, Erving. 2009. *Stigma: Notes on the Management of Spoiled Identity*. New York: Simon and Schuster.

Harrell-Bond, Barbara E. 1986. *Imposing Aid: Emergency Assistance to Refugees*. Oxford: Oxford University Press.

Hooks, Bell. 1990. *Yearning: Race, Gender and Cultural Politics*. South End: Bell Hooks.

International Organization for Migration. 2015. *World Migration Report 2015—Migrants and Cities: New Partnerships to Manage Mobility*. Geneva: IOM, Available online: http://publications.iom.int/system/files/wmr2015_en.pdf (accessed on 13 February 2019).

Martiniello, Marco. 2011. *La démocratie Multiculturelle, Citoyenneté, Diversité, Justice Sociale*. Paris: Presses de Sciences Po/La Bibliothèque du citoyen.

Martiniello, Marco. 2015. Immigrants, ethnicized minorities and the arts: a relatively neglected research area. *Ethnic and Racial Studies* 38: 1229–35. [CrossRef]

Martiniello, Marco. 2018. Local communities of artistic practices and the slow emergence of a "post-racial" generation. *Ethnic and Racial Studies* 41: 1146–62. [CrossRef]

Martiniello, Marco, and Jean-Michel Lafleur. 2008. 'Ethnic Minorities' Cultural Practices as Forms of Political Expression: A Review of the Literature and a Theoretical discussion on Music. *Journal of Ethnic and Migration Studies* 34: 1191–15. [CrossRef]

Martiniello, Marco, and Jean-Michel Lafleur. 2010. Si se peude! Music, Musicians and Latino Vote at the 2008 US Presidential Election. *Migrações* 7: 213–29.

Mattern, Mark. 1998. *Acting in Concert. Music, Community, and Political Action*. New Brunswick: Rutgers University Press.

May, Vanessa. 2013. *Connecting Self to Society: Belonging in a Changing World*. Hampshire: Palgrave Macmillan.

O'Neill, Maggie. 2008. Transnational refugees: The transformative role of art? *Forum: Qualitative Sozialforschung/Forum: Qualitative Social Research* 9: 59.

Pink, Sarah. 2009. *Doing Sensory Ethnography*. London: Sage Publications Ltd.

Reverseau, Anne. 2019. Presenting a city: Brussels and its subjective portraits. *Brussels Studies* [Online], General Collection, 132. Available online: http://journals.openedition.org/brussels/2407 (accessed on 13 February 2019). [CrossRef]

Rose, Tricia. 1991. "Fear of a Black Planet": Rap Music and Black Cultural Politics in the 1990s. *Journal of Negro Education* 60: 276–90. [CrossRef]

Rotas, Alex. 2012. From 'asylum-seeker' to 'British artist': How refugee artists are redefining British art. *Immigrants and Minorities* 30: 211–38. [CrossRef]

Roy, William. 2010. How Social Movements Do Culture. *International Journal of Political and Cultural Sociology* 23: 85–98. [CrossRef]

Roy, William G., and Timothy J. Dowd. 2010. What is Sociological about Music? *Annual Review of Sociology* 36: 183–203. [CrossRef]

Salzbrunn, Monika. 2014. How diverse is Cologne carnival? How migrants appropriate popular art spaces. *Identities* 21: 92–106. [CrossRef]

Schechner, Richard. 1985. *Between Theater and Anthropology*. Philadelphia: University of Pennsylvania Press.

Street, John. 2003. 'Fight the Power': The Politics of Music and the Music of Politics. *Government and Opposition* 38: 113–30. [CrossRef]

Tacchi, Jo. 1998. Radio Texture: Between Self and Others. In *Material Cultures: Why Some Things Matter*. Edited by Daniel Miller. London: University College London Press, pp. 25–46.
Vanderwaeren, Els. 2014. Integrating by means of art? Expressions of cultural hybridisations in the city of Antwerp. *Identities* 21: 60–74. [CrossRef]
Vertovec, Steven. 2007. Super-diversity and its implications. *Ethnic and Racial Studies* 30: 1024–54. [CrossRef]
Willner-Reid, Matthew. 2015. Emergence and Decline of a Protest Movement: The Anti- Deportation Campaign for Afghan Asylum Seekers in Belgium. *Journal of Refugee Studies* 28: 505–22. [CrossRef]

 © 2019 by the authors. Licensee MDPI, Basel, Switzerland. This article is an open access article distributed under the terms and conditions of the Creative Commons Attribution (CC BY) license (http://creativecommons.org/licenses/by/4.0/).

Article

Artists from Syria in the International Artworld: Mediators of a Universal Humanism

Cristina Cusenza

Institute of Social & Cultural Anthropology, University of Oxford, Oxford OX2 6PE, UK; cristina.cusenza@hotmail.com

Received: 10 January 2019; Accepted: 4 March 2019; Published: 29 March 2019

Abstract: With the outbreak of the Syrian conflict in 2011, many artists left as part of a massive migratory flow out of the country. Other artists had already migrated because of perceived constraints to art-making due to censorship and lack of professional opportunities. Both waves of migration converged in artistic hubs throughout the Middle East and Europe. From the interviews I carried out with visual artists from Syria displaced in London and other locations, it emerged that they faced a shared dilemma. Many wished to move away from politics focusing on *universal* themes like human suffering, which in the Syrian art-scene were perceived to be *apolitical*. In exile, however, it is precisely these themes that marked their works as political in the eyes of agents of the artworld and international audiences. I argue that this politicization is a form of essentialization and homogenization of the Syrian art-scene abroad, for categorizing these artists as 'Syrian' or 'Middle Eastern' flattens their individual creativity by placing them within a national or regional category. This form of 'othering' is rooted in the history of Western colonialism in the Middle East and postcolonial geopolitics and power relations structuring the Syrian conflict and Western perceptions of it. I show how my informants attempt to overcome these constraints by employing the discursive register of *universalism*, while often organizing their lives around the 'Syrian artist' category.

Keywords: Syrian artist; minority arts; universalism; political art

1. Introduction

Just two months after having worked as anesthetist in a Damascene hospital, Tarek Tuma, an aspiring painter from Douma, decided to start a new life in London. Beginning in 2005, he studied English for more than a year to allow himself to train as artist. He was accepted into The Art Academy and later graduated from the prestigious City & Guilds of London Art School. However, Tarek struggled economically. Having recently become an art history teacher in a primary school, his dream is to become a full-time artist.

In this thesis, I investigate dynamics at play for Syrian artists like Tarek, who are navigating the international, Western-centered artworld, having been displaced from their country and its artistic scene. I specifically concentrate on the tension between these artists' claims to mediate universal, apolitical themes, and the 'politicizing', essentialist discourses pervading the Western art industry. I will use the term 'visual artist' in an all-encompassing way, referring to someone who engages in artistic practice and exhibits in available platforms (via market or other routes), to avoid falling into an unreflecting collapsing of 'artist', 'anti-regime', 'activist', as generally assumed by literature written from a Western perspective.

With the outbreak of the conflict in 2011, following protests asking for the toppling of President Asad and a 'democratic shift' for Syria, most artists left as part of a massive migratory flow out. They converged in artistic hubs throughout the Middle East (Beirut, Dubai, Abu Dhabi, Doha, Bahrain) and, predominantly, Europe (Figure 1). Many anti-regime artists from older generations ended up in France and young talents in Germany (Griswold 2018). Artistic partnerships with France were established before the war because of available scholarships sponsored by French art institutions, installed in Syria since the colonial period[1]. Since 2011, many have found prolific platforms throughout France, mainly thanks to the association Syria.art. As for Germany, as a result of the open-door policies by Merkel's government in 2015, it represents a central hub for Syrian artists (Holmes and Castañeda 2016).

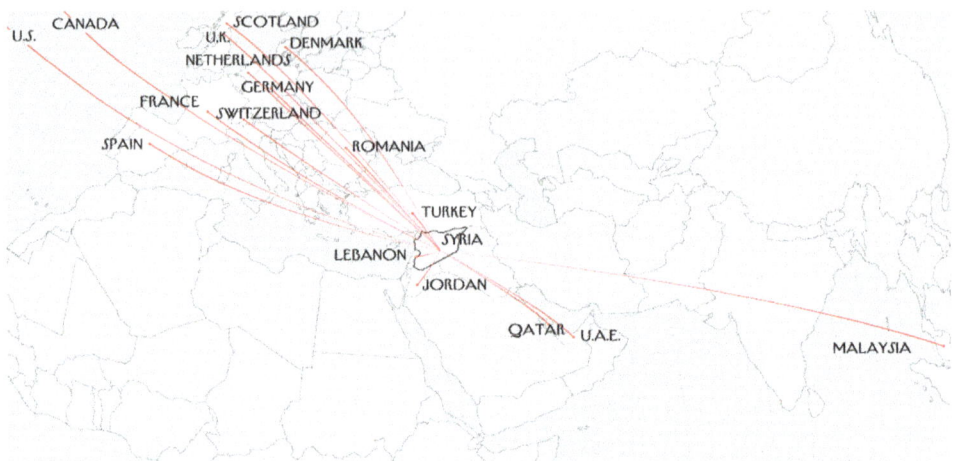

Figure 1. Map following the paths of a hundred artists who have fled Syria since 2011. Source: Griswold (2018), public domain image.

This phenomenon has intensified throughout the war and, as it stands now, the Syrian art-scene can be said to have mobilized out of the country's borders. The current situation of emergency in Syria—a site for proxy warfare—is dramatic: Beyond half of the population is in need of humanitarian assistance, the UN estimates that the number of killings is around 400,000, and there are approximately 5.6 million refugees abroad (UN News 2018). At the same time, other artists like Tarek left before 2011, because of perceived constraints to art-making due to censorship, but also lack of innovation in the arts and difficulty finding professional opportunities. This landscape is reflected in my informants' trajectories: Some moved abroad in the early 2000s to receive more 'sophisticated' training, and never returned, whilst others had to flee because of war and persecution. Greater accessibility of their works to wider audiences and, in some instances, an 'aesthetic adaptation' to the conflict, has given way, beyond their intentions, to the 'Syrian refugee art industry'. I contextualize these developments exploring dilemmas encountered by artists from Syria trying to emplace themselves in new artistic contexts: How does the Western-centered art-scape get configured in their eyes, in comparison to the Syrian one? What new demands and stereotypes do they confront, and how do they respond to them? Are artists asked to reflect on their practice in new ways? Do they use art to reflect on the conflict? How are their works received, and through what lenses are they interpreted? In other words, what is the social and political logics of being a Syrian artist today? These are important questions that I explore through my informants' perspectives. I am interested in the relationship between sociopolitical change and aesthetic transformation, and I hope to contribute to existing literature on 'artists at times of war'[2] through an anthropologically informed study of these artists' status. As I will discuss, this

---

[1]   Syria was a French Mandate 1919–1946.
[2]   See (Bevan 2015; Bourke 2017; Mackinlay 2003; Zinn 2011).

approach involves disentanglement from mainstream curatorial practices tending to homogenize 'Arab artists' under a regional category that has political connotations (Schneider 2017, p. 15).

Talking with my informants, I immediately encountered a refusal to communicate a political stance when asked to reflect on their art, which deserves investigation. Despite differences in style, themes, media used, backgrounds, and ethnic status, a common contradiction emerges for displaced Syrian artists. One the one hand, in Syria, visual artists tended to privilege abstract painting and depict 'universal' themes such as 'human suffering' to escape censorship, but also because they were thought to transcend politics, understood as taking a position with regard to concrete political players (i.e., the regime). However, to their own surprise, it is precisely these themes that, in exile, render their art 'political' for audiences, insofar as they perceive such focus on 'suffering' as an intervention in the conflict. Artists see such 'politicization' as 'trivialization' of their work connected to their shared uneasiness with the 'Syrian artist category' used to describe them. They perceive such identification, that posits them as 'Syrian'/'Middle Eastern' before 'artists', as forced because it values their identity over their talent. I attempt to bring light to, and eventually challenge, ideological frameworks behind such processes of homogenization, thus offering broader insights on the relatively peripheral place of 'minority-artists' in the international artworld.

I argue that my informants use a discursive strategy of 'universal humanism' when articulating the significance of their work and that they tend to distance their art from politics because their approaches are informed, to varying degrees, by the specific legacy concerning artists' relationship to the Syrian regime. This has often brought artists to 'suspend the political' and focus on themes considered *universal* and *apolitical*. When entering the Western-centered artworld, artists from Syria reclaim the 'autonomy' of their art in reaction to external interpretations that 'localize' their work, based on prevalent assumptions that the Syrian regime has hindered all forms of creativity as a result of oppression. These artists are also expected to visually represent the war, communicating their political positioning within it. I encourage focus on the fact that desires mapped into Syrian artists' production—by the art industry, its agents, and audiences—are shaped by geopolitical dynamics, namely the place of 'the West' in the conflict and historical presence in the region. I argue that the criterion for approaching Syrian art has changed from 'ethnicity' and 'location'—thought to be encapsulated in Arabic/Islamic calligraphy—to 'national identity' and 'politics'—expected to transpire from works dealing with current political events. Thus, what it means to be a 'Syrian artist' has changed, and a form of 'othering' continues being reproduced by the market. I show that the political relevance of art is not always the consequence of artists' choice, since they are embedded in complex networks and situated in a discursive space. More generally, I conclude that the artworld remains a highly contested site where cultural identity, political claims, and power relations are negotiated and re-inscribed. It will be seen that while most artists lament such categorization as 'Syrian' because it is 'flattening' their individual creativity, for some it reveals useful for emerging in a competitive marketplace. In fact, most are unable to escape it, because channels provided—galleries promoting 'Middle Eastern art', or exhibitions centered around national/regional political climate—tend to reinforce it. In the Conclusions, I reflect on future prospects for my informants, navigating between disillusionment and hope, as Syria has entered the eighth year of war.

Concerning my approach to my informants, I concentrated on their subjectivity and discourses, treating them as 'epistemic partners' (Given 2008), considering they have expertise to share—from first-hand experience of the Syrian art-scene, to knowledge of institutional dynamics of the artworld—while acknowledging the necessity to deconstruct the view that artists are detached from society.

2. Materials and Methods

This paper draws most of its ethnographic data from six weeks of fieldwork I conducted in London in the summer 2017. During this time, I met and interviewed six visual artists. As outlined, Tarek Tuma is a painter and art teacher; Hasan Abdalla is a painter, originally Kurdish, who fled

Syria because of persecution; Ammar Azzouz is an architect from Homs, now working as architect at the firm Arup; Hrair Sarkissian is an established photographer from Damascus; Issam Kourbaj is a conceptual artist in residence and Lector in Art at Cambridge; and Ibrahim Fakhri is an activist and graphic designer from Damascus. Carrying out semistructured, in-depth interviews with a topic-guide (see Appendix A) was meant to allow my informants to provide the information *they* think is important (Wolcott 2005, p. 160). All of them are fluent in English. I contacted them via email or Facebook, having come across their names in online searches, and I encountered positive responses from all of them through oral consent. This might be partly due to their 'aspiration of recognition or publicity', as Duclos notes in relation to Iraqi artists in Damascus who did not want to be anonymized (Duclos 2017, p. 4), as well as their motivation to share with wider audiences their ideas related to art but also, for some, to the revolution that first. Concerns for some of my informants included covering war-related trauma or 'politics', disclosing information that would put their families—still in Syria—at risk. I tried to handle these 'ethically important moments' (Guillemin and Gillam 2004, p. 265) by avoiding sensitive questions. However, on occasion, they would 'unintentionally' reveal details and requested anonymity. Throughout the paper, I reflect on my positionality as a Western researcher studying Middle Eastern artists and the challenges involved.

The only criteria I followed in selecting participants were artists' nationality, and the location where they are based (London)—'purposive sampling' (Bernard 2017, p. 14). This resulted in a diverse group of artists. My fieldwork consisted of repeated meetings, going to artists' exhibitions, visiting their houses/ateliers, etc. I also had the chance to talk with curators, as well as academics specialized in Syria, such as political scientist Wendy Pearlman and writer Malu Halasa.

As for my methodological choice of London as my main field-site, I adopted Candea's suggestion of re-valuing 'arbitrary locations', for it allows the ethnographer to appreciate the multi-sitedness, but also incompleteness, of any local context (Candea 2007, p. 172; Gellner 2012, p.11). London is 'arbitrary' as 'it bears no necessary relation to the wider object of study (Candea 2007, p. 180), the Syrian art-scene. Indeed, as I will discuss, the UK does not represent a central concentration point for Syrian artists. London is not a 'traditional village' but a metropolis and main global art center, within which I travelled to meet my informants.

When dealing with members of a population experiencing unprecedented migration out of the country, it might be argued that the most appropriate method is 'multi-sited ethnography', a necessary adaptation of the discipline to changing world realities, suited to the study of transnational communities (Marcus 1995; Gupta and Ferguson 1997). Existing literature on diasporas is extensive[3], including research on displaced artists from the Middle East, especially Iraqi (Shabout 2012), Egyptian (Winegar 2008a), Palestinian (Boullata 2004; De Cesari 2012; Salih and Richter-Devroe 2014), and Iranian (Naficy 1991; Walker-Parker 2005). I deal with individual, displaced professionals with different personal paths and approaches, rather than a unified community of artists, and my methodological choices respond to these conditions. Indeed, I carried out other six semistructured interviews through Skype to gauge an idea of the artistic scene in other hubs where Syrian artists are based. Of these, Houmam Al-Sayed is a popular painter working in Lebanon, Gregory Buchakjian is a Lebanese photographer and art historian specialized in Middle Eastern art, and Dima Nachawi is an illustrator and clown-performer based in Beirut. Jaber Al Azmeh—photographer from Damascus living in Qatar—, Tammam Azzam—who uses different media, currently working in Germany—, and Ammar Abd-Rabbo—photographer and journalist based in France since childhood—are among the most well-known contemporary artists from Syria. These interviews helped me to identify narratives common to exiled Syrian artists, and I encourage further research to enrich the data collected.

---

[3] See (Clifford 1997; Cohen 2008; Safran 1991; Wimmer and Glick-Schiller 2002).

3. Results and Discussion

3.1. The Booming Syrian Art-Scene

In the last decade or so, before the 2011 protest movement, public media, the internet, and the international artworld have been putting the spotlight on 'the emerging Syrian art-market' (Anderson and Duncan 2010). Statements such as 'Syria is liberalizing its economy, foreign capital is flooding into the country, and contemporary art is booming' (DP News 2010) have been making the pages of Western newspapers, art blogs, and magazines, and websites of auction houses such as Sotheby's and Christie's, installed in Dubai since 2005. Since the early 2000s, these have claimed that art produced in the Middle East will find favor with Western collectors (Seaman 2016). As for Syria, the Ayyam gallery, founded in 2006, is considered the most successful in terms of primary and secondary market presence (Duncan 2010; Oweis 2010).

The perceived 'latedness' of Syria in entering the international market is partly connected to 'Western misperceptions about the extent and nature of its authoritarian regime' (Kluijver 2009). The process of institutionalization of art in Syria is considered still in its infancy in comparison to that of other countries in the region. Works by contemporary Syrian artists feature considerably less than those by Egyptian, Iranian, Lebanese, and Iraqi artists, and from the Gulf states, in auctions and exhibitions in the West—such as, among recent ones, 'Unveiled: New art from the Middle East' (London 2009), 'Golden Gates: New Art from the Middle East' (Paris 2009), and 'Come Invest In Us. You'll Strike Gold' (Vienna 2012). Works by Syrians that have sold the most are by older generations (Kräussl 2014, p. 12). The opening of Ayyam—and other galleries such as Al Sayyed, Atassi, Tajallyat, Kalemaat, Free Hand, and Art House Syria—facilitated 'the privatisation and professionalization' of the art-scene in Syria (Woodcock 2012, p. 4). Under Hafiz Al-Asad, the government used to be the main cultural entrepreneur, establishing relations of tutelage with artists in a closed, socialist economy, whilst neoliberal measures implemented by Bashar have favored the emergence of a private sector in the arts, yet still controlled (Longuenesse and Roussel 2014, p. 30).

While I am not going to focus on the political context that determined conditions of production preceding this booming, I briefly explore how this legacy has informed predominant understandings of the relationship between art, politics, and the market among contemporary Syrian visual artists.

3.2. Artists' Political Positionality

The typological schema proposed by Abbas (2005) helps to broadly understand visual artists' positionality in relation to the regime, including those sustaining the 'Official Ideology', 'Conformists', 'Others', and 'Those on the Opposition'[4].

It can be seen that there is a clear polarization. At the center of the schema are artists following the Baathist party and its allied ones under the coalition of the National Progressive Front, who adopt a figurative, realist style celebrating Arabic heritage and the president as 'Arab leader' (Figures 2 and 3)—among these, Mamdûh Qachelâna, Hilmi Sabûnî, and Ghazi Al-Khalidi, President of the Artists' Trade Union, and Naji Obeid and Osama Jahjah, using Arabic calligraphy.

---

[4] Please check (Abbas 2005) at: https://books.openedition.org/ifpo/564?lang=en.

Figure 2. What the Arabs brought to Europe. (Oil on Canvas.) Source: Al-Khalidi (1990), open access.

Figure 3. Grand-scale mural staging Syria's victory over Israel in the Yom Kippur War in lieu of defeat (n.d.). Damascus, Syria: October War Panorama Museum. Source: Stone Fish (2013), open access.

On the other hand, Abbas identifies artists on the opposition—'circle of artists-activists', including Ahmad Moualla, Nazir Ismail, artists exiled in Europe such as Sakher Farzât, Bachar al-'Îssâ, and Najah al-Bukai, and the most representative case of Youssef Abdelke, member of the Communist Party, imprisoned for years because of caricatures of public authorities (Abbas 2005, p. 50). In general, it emerged that state-sponsored painters are dismissed by cultural elites as 'inauthentic by dint of their association with the government' (Shannon 2005, p. 377). In a way, it might be argued that I reproduce such discourses, delimiting my focus to artists not aligned with the regime, and relying on sources written from a Western, tendentially anti-regime perspective. I want to avoid falling into an analytically unreflecting collapsing of 'artist' and 'anti-regime'. In fact, Abbas points out that artists supporting the regime are not 'aesthetically conformists' (Abbas 2005, p. 18)—i.e., they do not necessarily reproduce precepts of the main ideology. 'Propaganda art', anyway, has been extensively used by the regime since its very beginning, an example being Nizâr Sabûr's gigantic portraits of President Hafiz (ibid., p. 35). Furthermore, Abbas notes that many artists have safeguarded a neutral position. This broad, stratified group includes those claiming not to be interested in politics and those exhibiting a 'cold, anti-conformist violence' (ibid., p. 52), such as Sara Shamma, internationally known for her images of anguished human bodies. As I will show, when entering the international scene, such 'experience of suffering' depicted by artists like Shamma will be interpreted as political statements.

I discussed with Tarek the multilayered engagements of artists with the establishment:

> Until now you have pro-regime artists, but also those refusing to take sides. If you're a neutral artist, you're either afraid of the regime or you're with it, and in that case you wouldn't want to reveal your position now.

Yet, regardless of their political views, he would evaluate these artists' work 'as pieces of art in themselves', citing the distinctively 'Syrian', 'neutral' style of Safwan Dahoul, one of the most popular painters, known since the 80s for his 'Dream' series featuring distressed female figures[5].

Art commentators in the West such as Mayamanah Farhat tend to think that pervading themes in Syrian artists' production remain 'abstracted, distorted studies of the human figure or commentary on recent political events' (Woodcock 2012, p. 25). It is worth noting that throughout the second part of the 20th century, 'the European tripartite system of private galleries, public museums and independent journalistic criticism' (Lenssen 2014, p. 17) was not available in Syria, and absence of artistic criticism is unhelpful in fostering the popularity of art in society. Moreover, to have their work exhibited, artists have been required to avoid 'controversial' subject-matters (Cooke 2007, p. 9). It is after a severe economic crisis in the first decade of Hafiz's rule that public institutions progressively relied on sanctions on artists, bringing to the disappearance of the peaceful relationship between artists and state (Boëx 2011, p. 140; Becker 2005, p. 79). Under Hafiz, the state acted as the only sponsor and main educator in the arts on a Soviet model (Cooke 2007, p. 21), benefitting only those who accepted the boundaries specified by the Ministry of Information, and against which a 'transgressive counter culture' developed (Weeden 2015, p. 89). This resulted from the production of cartoons, plays, films, and novels in which 'dissident' artists engaged for decades. One of my informants pointed out that 'symbolic political messages were already in artworks, but they might have been ignored or not understood by everyone', citing Ali Ferzat's work[6]. In general, it can be said that a claim to 'political neutrality' and a tendency towards abstraction and symbolism is predominant in the visual arts. In order to understand my informants' positionality, I adopt Abbas' approach in considering aspects such as 'the self-judgment of the artist', 'their production', and their 'political behaviour' (Abbas 2005, p. 13). Indeed, I mainly focus on the discursive, rather than aesthetic, aspect of art.

It is with the 2011 uprisings that there has been an explosion of 'revolutionary cultural production' in Syria (Cooke 2016, p. 8). The protests are seen as the culmination of perceived oppression under Assad, use of physical violence by security forces against civilians, and silencing of civil rights (Hokayem 2013; Sottimano 2016, p. 458). They also need to be contextualized within wider regional tensions: The rise of political Islamism, waves of popular discontent manifested in the Arab Spring across the Middle East, economic deprivation, struggle for regional dominance between Iran and other Arab states, etc. (Foley 2013, p. 33; Abbas 2014, p. 52). Syrian society can be said to be divided between those opposing the regime—Sunni Muslims, members of minorities, working classes, rural populations, civilians who took up arms (Free Syrian Army)—and those wanting to preserve it or who feared alternatives, including 'crony capitalists', urban government employees, and other members of minorities (Pearlman 2017, p. xlii; Foley 2013, p. 42).

Not all artists got involved in the protests, from those few who came out publicly to back the President[7], to those who kept quiet, as they did not believe meaningful changes would have been

---

[5] See: http://www.ayyamgallery.com/artists/safwan-dahoul/images.
[6] Because of his caricatures of politicians, Farzat had his hands shattered in 2011 by security forces. He is now exiled in Kuwait (Halasa 2012).
[7] Included in the Facebook page 'Syrian List of Shame' (Little 2011).

achieved, to those who, like Jaber, decided 'not to go in the streets' in order to protect their families. His story is emblematic, for he first engaged in art when the revolution started:

> In such circumstances everybody has to give something to the people: the doctor will help the wounded, the baker make bread for whoever needs it, and the artist produce to report this history.

Jaber realized his first series, 'Wounds' (2012), of shots depicting blood-red and black silhouettes of figures in motion, represented 'people fighting bravely for their freedom'. In the same spirit, he produced in secret the series 'The Resurrection' (2014) (Figure 4), where civil society members hold the official newspaper (Al-Ba'ath) on which each wrote something against the regime, in the style of 'Facebook status'.

Figure 4. Detail from 'The Resurrection' (2014) by Jaber. (Printed on Cotton Rag Fine Art Archival paper.) London, UK: British Museum. Photograph by the author.

Active anti-regime artists received threats, had to remain silent or were forced into exile (Boëx 2013, p. 15)—among them, Hasan, who joined protests since the beginning, and was arrested in 2011 and tortured. Once out of prison, he fled illegally to England. He later learnt that his house had been raided by the police, and his son arrested.

As for Ibrahim's involvement in the protests, despite being already outside Syria, he devised a way to contribute to 'the revolution': Graffiti, such as the banner featuring faces of martyrs exhibited in Rich Mix, London (2013). Online platforms allowed him to circulate stencils for protesters.

In the case of Tammam, he managed to overcome a major logistical issue—the destruction of his studio in Damascus—by shifting from painting to digital media. The latter has become increasingly popular in 'post-Arab Spring countries', employed by artists such as Khalil Younes and Fares Cachoux (Al-Shami 2016). Tammam's 'Freedom Graffiti' print (2013), part of the 'Syrian Museum' series, went viral on social media (Figure 5).

Figure 5. Tammam's 'Freedom Graffity' (2013). (Digital Print.) Used by permission of the artist.

Such emotional intensity caused by this turbulent moment induced artists to shift the content of their art. Anti-regime voices received most attention in Western media, being celebrated as 'defiant art', having a misleading impact on the ways in which all art from Syria is seen. Since then, the 'emerging Syrian art-scene' has been bustling outside Syria to a greater extent: A profound shift occurred from a neoliberalization of the art market supported by the regime, to a concomitant anti-regime politicization and commercialization of artists' works abroad. I will now explore how these developments and the experience of displacement have informed my informants' subjectivities.

3.3. Othering 'the Syrian' before 'the Artist'

Flipping through art catalogues with Tarek and Ammar at P21 gallery in London, I observed I had not been able to find sources about visual art from Syria, and they explained that the lack of such books is a reflection of the absence of a unified Syrian cultural elite.

We met there as they wanted to show me where the first collective exhibition in which they participated took place, back in 2013. Tarek was lead curator of #WithoutWords: Emerging Syrian artists, for which artworks were smuggled out of Syria, by artists based abroad or still living there, many of whom were persecuted—Ali Ferzat and the Lens Young Collective. A more recent occasion where their works were shown was the exhibition 'Art of Resilience' at the US Embassy in London (January 2017). The organization Mosaic, together with the Asfari Foundation, played a major role in supporting Syrian artists in London, hosting public auctions of artworks, and sharing funds raised between artists and activity of aid relief. Since 2011, similar initiatives have been put in place, such as those by the Shubbak festival, International Alert and the British Red Cross. The general public's attention to 'Syrian art' might have also been stimulated by art-therapy projects set up by charities such as the London Art Therapy Centre, Flourish Foundation, and Refugee Week. However, Tarek and

Ammar noted that many organizations 'aren't active at the moment', and Ibrahim feels that Mosaic 'became one of those charities after the money'. Further, the London branch of Ayyam gallery closed down soon after its opening in 2013, because of 'the absence of fertile grounds in Europe for Middle Eastern art', as remarked by one of my informants.

My informants invited me to reflect on how media, public, and art collectors' attention to art produced by Syrian artists has declined, In fact, most articles and interviews of Syrian artists date back to the war's early years (2011–2014). I am going to explore reasons behind the initial enthusiasm for the 'phenomenon of Syrian art', in order to contextualize its fading appeal (and production). I look at discourses and practices that surround these artists and are beyond their control. I problematize the category of 'Syrian artist' conflated within that of 'Middle Eastern or Arab'. Homogenizing narratives weigh on non-Western artists in general yet evolve from a discrimination based on 'ethnicity' to a more subtle form of 'othering' because of changing geopolitical dynamics. This involves a shift from 'a culturally exotic other' to 'a politically exotic other supposed to be either exiled from or critical about his/her country of origin' (Araeen et al. 2002, p. 333). I argue that such essentializing tendencies are fostered precisely by Syrian artists' 'universalizing' discourses about their art.

It is useful to adopt the notion of 'artworld' as imbricated networks involving differently positioned actors, in order to study 'the discursive practices that determine who will find a place within it' (Harris 2012b, p. 153). Despite celebrated 'pluralization' of the artworld in terms of origin of its actors (Elkins et al. 2010, p. 14; Schultheis et al. 2016, p. 18), access to it seems to depend on artists' 'positionality vis-à-vis various hegemonies and ideologies at play, regionally and internationally' (Toukan 2013, p. 75). That is, the political situation in Syria, Western countries' position in it, and their historical presence in the region determine the ways in which Syrian artists' work is interpreted. In other words, 'the particularities of place' (Harris 2012b, p. 16) do not simply have a geographical dimension and still determine patterns of inclusion/exclusion in the artworld, whose centers of gravity remain Western art institutions/metropolis. Despite growing interest for non-Western forms of contemporary art such as African, Middle Eastern, and Chinese, these artists remain powerless players. On the one hand, 'art always takes place within a national situation' in terms of audiences, museums, and parameters within which it can take place (Elkins 2007, p. 16). During our conversation at Something Gallery, where Hasan's works were exhibited, the curator expressed her discomfort with the Scottish Cultural Secretary's statement that 'artists don't have to be close to government, they just have to have a common understanding of what the country wants' (Wade 2017). Moreover, artists often choose to give a sense of their 'localised' identity in their work, and yet, a 'methodological nationalism' cannot be adopted to the study of the art-scape in which they operate, since it has become an increasingly international enterprise (Belting and Buddensieg 2009, p. 10; Gardner and Green 2013).

Whenever my informants perceive that their art is dismissed as 'Syrian', they feel their talent is overlooked. They are aware that the 'straitjacket of geography and prescribed identities' (Carver 2006) weighing on them comes with imaginations about Syria and the wider region via association with war and displacement, as expressed by Ibrahim. Based in the UK for the past fifteen years, in addition to his involvement in art-activism, Ibrahim works fulltime as graphic designer for Alaraby TV Network and is also a curator. In London, 'there have been attempts to create a network of Syrian artists' and to find more platforms for those scattered throughout Europe. Ibrahim is one of the collaborators of 'Syria Speaks: Art and Activism from the front line' (2014), committed to bringing to the fore the voices of artists and musicians denouncing the 'untold bloodshed' taking place in Syria, who cannot emerge 'because of politics'. Moreover, as I was able to grasp in my conversation with Gregory—the Lebanese art historian—investment in Syrian art has collapsed within the region itself, because 'Arab states are in deep political crises'.

These observations refer to those ideological frameworks shaping selection and evaluation of artworks, which are never neutral (Winegar 2008b, p. 652). Exhibiting and museum practices have a historical and institutional dimension, often shaping audiences' perceptions (Karp and Lavine 1991, p. 12).

Before exploring this further, a note of contextualization on such debates on the status of 'minority arts' in the international artworld is necessary. In the 1980s, many took issue with the exclusion of non-Western artists and the neglect of their contribution to 'mainstream developments' (Araeen et al. 2002, p. 333). These sensibilities seek to 'retrace modern art in other parts of the world' (Elkins 2007, p. 21) and are part of wider efforts in academia to disentangle from hegemonic interpretative tools of historicism and Eurocentrism (Chakrabarty 2000, 2009). In anthropology, there has been a shift from a view of art objects as 'emblems of holistic cultures', unlocking the worldview of so-called 'ethnic' communities (Kaur and Dave-Mukherji 2014, p. 7; Welsch 2004, p. 403), to the study of individual artists as legitimate subjects of inquiry, a path initiated by Schneider (1996, p. 184). Appadurai argues that early approaches entailed the 'metonymic freezing' of natives by their places (Appadurai 1988, p. 36). Instead, I hope to demonstrate that 'taking seriously individuality and idiosyncratic discourses' does not imply neglecting social processes in which artists are embedded (Schneider 1996, p. 188). A sound anthropological analytical strategy goes beyond the modernist myth of the hyper-subjectivity of the artistic genius, appreciating that artists never operate in isolation from economic and sociopolitical domains (Krauss 1986, p. 4; Langton and Papastergiadis 2003, p. 13). However, the art establishment often undermines individual talent of minority-artists, expected to reveal elements of cultural 'distinctiveness' (Harris 2012b, p. 162; Belting and Buddensieg 2009, p. 40). As noted by Araeen et al. (2002, p. 340), founder of the 'Third Text' journal, and by Taylor (1994), the system of exclusions at the basis of 'modern art' has been refined by multiculturalism, centered around the importance of recognizing 'cultural others', still based on an assimilationist logic, and concealed by a universalist frame (Araeen et al. 2002).

For Syrian/Middle Eastern artists forms of 'othering' are structured around orientalist assumptions:

> Tarek: If the Arabic culture was valued, its art would also be valued ... But it's still debated whether it's art or not. Fortunately, they now teach this in schools in Europe.

Edward Said famously conceptualized 'Orientalism' as the positioning of 'the Orient' as backwards because of Western imperialism in these territories (1978). This phenomenon seems to have escalated in recent years. According to Gregory, since 9/11 and the 'war on terror', 'the whole world became interested in Middle Eastern art practices' (Buchakjian 2012, p. 40). Art agents, pushed by funding bodies, looked for intellectual/artistic sources as containers of knowledge about the Arab world. Concurrently, Gulf States started investing in art, creating 'a contradictory situation: on one side, Arabs associated with terrorists, and on the other, Arabs with money'.

I suggest that the recent exhibition 'Age of Terror: Art since 9/11' at the IWM in London reproduces these discourses since it puts together a collection of works by Middle Eastern artists highlighting controversial feelings post-9/11 in the region. I observed a similar tendency to group artists from the diverse Arab region in the exhibition 'Living Histories. Recent acquisitions of works on paper by contemporary Arab artists' in Room 34, 'The Islamic World' of the British Museum. The series 'Resurrection' by Jaber, Issam's installation 'Dark Water, Burning World' and a drawing by Houmam Al-Sayed (2009) feature in it. The issue at play in putting this exhibition of contemporary artists inside the Islamic art section is the conflation of region, culture, history, and religion (Winegar 2008b, p. 655). Sharing the same birthplace or having a name that identifies them 'as having hailed' from a place is not simply a nominalist definition (Withey 2013, p. 16). Gupta and Ferguson remind us that all associations of place, people, and culture are 'social and historical creations to be explained, not given natural facts' (Gupta and Ferguson 1997, p. 4). In this setting, Winegar would argue, a discontinuum is established between a glorious, past Islamic civilization and a present status of decay. However, 'Arabic' and 'Islamic' are not to be conflated, since the Middle East has contested borders, subsuming various ethnic/religious groups (Roudi-Fahimi and Kent 2007). Critically, I argue that a shift in focus from 'ethnicity' and 'location' to 'national identity' and 'politics' as criterion for approaching 'Arab art' has occurred; that is, from 'ethnographic' Islamic calligraphy to works dealing with current politics. As my informants invited me to reflect, qualifying art in this way is problematic:

Tammam: I would like to have more sponsors, but not because of my nationality. I want to be seen as an artist *and* Syrian, not because I'm a refugee who's able to paint.

As a Western researcher dealing with artists originally from the Middle East, I have approached my informants with the expectation of finding 'counter-hegemonic statements' in their art: This is not a completely unfounded presumption if one looks at Syria's artistic history, especially post-2011 'revolutionary art'. However, when researching art produced in conditions of crisis, during wartime or under siege, celebrating it as 'anti-powers resistance' involves predetermining its dramatic dimensions (Spyer in Kaur and Dave-Mukherji 2014, p. 73; Boullata 2004, p. 75), assuming that all artists are against the regime. The tendency to give prominence to sociopolitical conditions determining artists' production involves making epistemological statements about their capacity to overcome them (Marcus and Myers 1995, p. 5). The imposition of such a frame comes from the fact that Syria as a location is imbued with historical/political content.

As a reply to my first email, Hrair said he did not want to be categorized as Syrian artist, as he is 'not committed to the Syrian art-scene (. . .) the only thing we have in common is where we're from'. Others insisted I would make sure their name was not going to be 'associated' to that of others, while featuring in the same research. They all took issue with the 'refugee moniker' defining them. I therefore appreciated the arbitrariness of the 'exiled Syrian artists' category, unsettling my initial research focus, which shifted to *whether* and *how* displaced artists from Syria reflect on the conflict through their creative practices and how they react to the label used to describe them. My expectation of finding a 'diasporic community' is to be related to romanticized online accounts of the 'Syrian artistic diaspora'. These refer to artists–activists like Ibrahim and Dima, committed to promoting change through human-rights organizations, opposition groups, etc. (Qayyum 2011, p. 8; Chaudhary and Moss 2016, p. 15), or to the smaller, transnational network of more established artists—including Tammam, Houmam, Jaber, and Ammar Abd Rabbo—whose works are brought together by internationally travelling exhibitions. As for London, however, I found a fragmented, non-existent Syrian art-scene: My informants were barely able to mention names of other Syrian artists living there. I have come under the impression that in Lebanon, France, and Germany, relations among Syrian artists are more settled. Yet, Tammam, completing a fellowship at the Institute for Advanced Study in Delmonhost, expressed his uneasiness with the 'superficial trend of Syrian art' in Germany. Similarly, Houmam—based in Beirut, 'the *de facto* capital of the Syrian contemporary art-scene' (Brownell 2014)—does not consider himself 'a fun of local art circles', including the Syrian one, which remains separate.

Different factors explain the lack of collaborations between artists—competition, diverging approaches to art, institutional, financial or personal issues, as well as political ones, including migration policies. My initial assumption can be said to reproduce social scientists' tendency to overstate internal homogeneity of transnational communities (Wimmer and Glick-Schiller 2002, p. 233). Indeed, a 'methodological nationalism' has affected the study of migrants, including 'diaspora artists', approached primarily in relation to their homeland (Wimmer and Glick-Schiller 2002, p. 228; Anthias 1998; Deebi 2012, p. 12). Exhibitions such as 'Word into art: Artists of the modern Middle East' (Porter 2006), and 'Unveiled: New art from the Middle East' (Farjam 2009) presented works by Egyptian, Iranian, Iraqi, Palestinian, Lebanese, and (proportionally less) Syrian artists as unitary phenomena. 'Diaspora as creative space' essentializes artists. The term 'transmigrants' captures more fully the complexity of their accommodation and resistance to hegemonic contexts (Glick-Schiller et al. 1992), as it is rooted in a conceptualization of identity as intersectional, 'mobile and unstable relation of difference' (Gupta and Ferguson 1997, p. 13; Anthias 1998), which resonates with my informants', who attempt to resist imposed categories, emphasizing their flexible disposition. This has implications for methods used and forms of knowledge produced.

3.4. The Discursive Strategy of 'Universalism'

Through my fieldwork, I was able to grasp that the Orientalism weighing on Middle Eastern artists is obscured, as Withey (2013) argues, by the predominant discourse of *universalism*, embraced by

Syrian artists, who present themselves as mediators as a 'universal humanism', and by Western viewers and curators, but with different motivations. The latter promote Syrian artists as universal because of their capacity to criticize their 'troubled, sectarian society' and to embrace 'Western values' such as cosmopolitanism, respect for human rights, etc. (Groys 2008, p. 181). Art critics seem to expect Syrian artists' work to 'have a political edge', as much as contemporary Tibetan artists are expected to reproduce a narrative on Chinese Colonialism (Harris 2012b, p. 159). They are, however, required to express these issues in a visual vocabulary catered to the market: Conceptual art. I had the chance to talk with a curator, Rebecca, who reproduced this narrative:

> The West wants Middle Eastern artists, but the region is so unstable that the plan of bringing Western art-making there isn't happening. Its art is becoming so precious because it survives conflict.

On the gallery's website, Hasan's canvases are defined as 'visually, culturally and historically unique', communicating a 'quiet sense of yearning'. Rebecca was attracted by Hasan's art as she could 'feel happy memories of the Middle East' despite the trauma experienced, making his art 'universally appealing' (Figure 6).

Figure 6. In September 2017, Hasan titled this painting 'Friends' (n.d.), but recently re-posted it on Facebook as 'Agony in the Streets', making me wonder whether Rebecca's description would have changed. (Acrylic on canvas.). Used by permission of the artist.

Whenever artists like Hasan are thought to transmit universal messages, or the uniqueness of their 'culturally-specific styles' is emphasized, a discourse of 'othering' is reproduced. On the other hand, I argue that the way in which my informants use such a 'universalist narrative' differs, because they see the themes they depict as transcending politics. Their way of including themselves within a universal category of artists through an emphasis on individualism is a 'creative strategy' (Harris 2012a, p. 234) to resist imposition of imagined constructions of 'Syrianness'. And while my informants seek to achieve global visibility, they do not necessarily emulate 'Western mainstream'. Moreover, they are aware that 'difference has become marketable' and they can actively 'perform ethnicity' and 'export themselves' (Mosquera in Langton and Papastergiadis 2003, p. 19; Kaur and

Dave-Mukherji 2014, p. 10). Indeed, the fragile human figure recurring in the visual arts in Syria, as much as 'the refugee', entrapped Syrians and their destroyed cities, come to represent the very 'symbolic capital', an 'iconography of suffering' that makes them aesthetically recognizable to curators.

Some artists—like Issam, in the UK since the 1990s—embrace the 'Syrian identification', yet maintaining an 'authentic' stance:

> Because I'm from that part of the world, everything's charged differently. Sometimes I cannot escape it. But that's my landscape and my job as artist is to present it in a way that can be digested.

Who needs to learn how to 'digest' the suffering caused by war? Is it Western audiences, not familiar to these realities, or Syrians themselves? Issam made this observation during his talk at King's College (October 2017). Ammar expressed similar thoughts:

> Every piece of art is about politics. Syria is always on my mind, and as creative person I must, and I have the power to, do something for Syrians there.

For Issam and Ammar, it is about accepting 'the inevitability of exile art to be political' (Homsey 2016, p. 8), that is, the *diaspora position*. There seems to be a general understanding that Syrian artists are the most entitled, by virtue of their origin, to do so. These perceptions are to be reconnected to controversies around instances of 'cultural appropriation' in the arts, particularly when Western artists adopt styles/themes considered to appertain to another 'culture'[8]. Arguably, in some cases, artists unintentionally 'bestow a status as others on them' (Schneider 1996, p. 184), because it is precisely what they think makes them 'universal'—the theme of human suffering—that marks them as 'particular'.

In his book, Gregory argues that 'Middle Eastern artists' 'shift to the domestic is a manifestation of a renewed Orientalism', with the difference that 'local artists have replaced European Orientalists in producing the iconography' (Buchakjian 2012, p. 79). In other words, my informants might be self-ascribing the category of 'other' simply by referring to the situation in Syria. Critically, they might not be conscious of it, because 'it's the way in which the West mediatizes their work that politicises it', as Gregory observed. In artists' view, such 'politicisation' is perceived as a 'trivialisation', preventing attribution of transformative capacities to their art (Jelinek 2013, p. 10). Because of this context, my informants differentiate their work from, in Gregory's words, 'a strategic production since 2011, that's not a deep reflection on what's going on'. One may recall predominant understandings of art as 'socially relevant', 'authentic' practice. In 2011, Abdelke urged younger generations of artists to be skeptical of the new market's 'financial attractions', because the artworks promoted do not reflect the rich Syrian visual heritage (Takieddine 2011, p. 60).

Dima is critical of the corporate-oriented mentality around which 'Western art agencies', particularly in the UK, are structured, which she learned about during her studies at Kings College (London). Such perceived limitations brought Dima to move back to Lebanon, where working as free-lancer artist is more feasible; she is a 'clown performer' for the initiative 'Clown me in', committed to providing relief to disadvantaged communities. As it emerged from my interviews, the greatest challenge for artists is to 'emancipate themselves from big players of the global art-market' (Schultheis et al. 2016, p. 256). Moreover, as noted by Tarek, works for exhibitions are often selected dependently on curators' personal preferences/contacts, 'being treated as commodities'. Tarek's conception of art resonates with that of older generations, as he developed his approach in Syria before the 'booming'. This concern that adjusting one's choices to the market's demands might compromise 'authenticity' of the sentiments inspiring artworks is shared by Syrian artists (Shannon 2005, p. 378), as well as in the Western world.

---

[8] See (Ziff and Rao 1997; Young 2010).

At the same time, artists are not always able to be in control of the ways in which their artworks circulate in the 'already saturated visual-discursive space' (Malmvig 2016, p. 264). Hrair recounted that in 2011 journalists from the Netherlands and the US contacted him to post images from his series 'Execution Squares' on newspapers, 'relating them to the conflict, as critique of the ongoing killings, while it has nothing to do with that because Syria has become an incomparable execution square'. Hrair realized the series in 2008. It comprises photographs of squares in Aleppo, Latakia and Damascus, taken at dawn, when people used to be hanged because of civil punishment. He came up with this project as a consequence of a tormenting vision: At the age of twelve, he saw 'three naked hanged bodies in the middle of a square wrapped with sheets that had their name and crime committed written on them' (Figure 7).

Figure 7. From Hrair's 'Execution Squares' (2008). (Archival inkjet print). Used by permission of the artist.

Similarly, Tammam laments mediatic manipulations of his biography, such as his presumed imprisonment and escape from Syria. While he has the 'refugee' status, Tammam 'travelled normally by plane' when leaving Damascus in 2011. For this reason, he refused to be interviewed by anyone except me in the past months, as I was not doing a 'journalistic report'. The context to which Hrair (Figure 8) and Tammam refer is exemplified by another instance—the exhibition 'Syria: a conflict explored', which went on in IWM venues across the UK in 2017—where, according to Hrair, the conflict is 'fetishized'. This is because photographs exhibited were taken by a Russian photographer 'who probably had easy access to Aleppo' and 'made them look dramatic'. He was also struck by the organization of a reception 'with people drinking all dressed up, a musician playing from the sound of bombs, while an entire nation is suffering'.

Figure 8. Hrair at the Tate Gallery, London. Photographs by the author.

3.5. Making Compromises

When navigating such complex space of the artworld, specifically in Europe, not everyone can choose to opt out from orientalist depictions. Artists may realize that 'collectivizing' their art may give them more chances to 'emerge', thus limiting to the discursive sphere contestation of imposed localization. The kind of identity bringing them together is a universal one, as the suffering they illustrate is an affective need rather than a political statement. However, as Harris (2006, p. 710) notes, rather than being free agents travelling internationally, artists' physical mobility is often limited: As Dima was able to grasp from her short staying in London, Syrian artists operate within 'strong Arab connections' that remain a separate circuit. Emplacing oneself in the competitive London art-scene is challenging, as Tarek explained:

> We're going to a warehouse where my paintings are stored. It's not the appropriate place where to keep them. Their journey is a reflection of the condition of art from Syria: if it was valued, it wouldn't be in a food storage.

Tarek has several unsold paintings, many of which he had to leave behind 'everywhere he moved in the UK'. Similarly, during his first months in London, Hasan used to live in a tiny flat, with walls covered with canvases he managed to bring with him from Syria. Some of my informants have concurrently other jobs, and some donated works to charities.

As seen, these artists' choices are not only driven by economic preoccupations, but also ethical concerns connected to representation of war, uneasiness with external categorization as

'Syrian', and commodification of artworks required by the market. I have also discussed how my informants *discursively* and *practically* mediate between *universality*—i.e., make their works accessible to international audiences—and *particularity*—representing a 'local situation' that is currently a war-zone. Yet, identification as 'Syrian' is not necessarily their 'curse' but may also represent their 'salvation', allowing some to find a place in the market.

4. Epilogue—Inhabiting Uncertainty

Now in the eighth year of the conflict, the shared impulse of responding to it with urgency seems to have vanished, as reflected in artworks produced and broader resolutions adopted by artists from Syria (Malmvig 2016, p. 258). Most of my informants are now working on new projects. Jaber realized the series 'Border-lines' in 2016 (Figure 9):

> Maybe it's a self-defense-mechanism, but seeing my country destroyed and people killing each other for nations, I don't believe in borders anymore. It's surreal that a Syrian cannot escape war because of a paperbook.

This abandonment of notions of 'national belonging' seems common to my informants and translates into indifference to changing location, to be related to the discourse of 'universalism' that they embrace. Hasan and Tarek articulated a tension between a 'cosmopolitan stance' and emotional bonds to homeland:

> H: 'In spite of jail and persecution, I still feel attached to Syria. But I wasn't angry when I came here, I adapted easily. I go to Costa to have coffee, as I used to do in Syria—it's funny, it reminds me of home.'

> T: 'This feeling of living in exile will always stay with me. But you recreate your identity abroad, I feel more cosmopolitan. Of course everyone's attached to family and friends, but in terms of country, I've abandoned it to live in peace.'

I could also perceive a shared sense of fear that the 'Syrian culture' would disappear. When entering the warehouse where Tarek's paintings are stored, I noticed a display-cabinet with food products exported from Syria. He suggested taking a photograph, as if these represented 'relics' of a lost past (Figure 10).

(a)

Figure 9. *Cont.*

(**b**)

Figure 9. Jaber's 'Nationalism 1' (**a**) and 'Survival 13' (**b**) (2016). 'Border-lines'. (Printed on cotton rag fine art archival paper.) Used by permission of the artist.

Figure 10. Display cabinet with Syrian goods. Photograph by the author.

My informants expressed disillusionment in relation to Syria's future. As it stands now, the multidimensional character of conflict seems to prevent taking any collective action that will guarantee ceasefire and rehabilitation (Vignal 2012; Heydemann 2013, p. 71). Houmam claimed that everyone has stopped believing in anything, from politics to religion: 'maybe only in fifty years, when I'm not going to be there, things might change'. As a result, he shifted his aesthetic focus from 'citizen zero' to 'citizen −1, −2 . . . since we're below average (of respect of human rights)'.

Hrair described the status in which Syrians find themselves as 'the opposite of hope, the condition of having nothing to hold onto'. In his video work 'Horizon' (2016) (Figure 11), he traces refugees' routes crossing the Mediterranean from Turkey to Greece, noting that 'only uncertainty accompanies them'.

Figure 11. From Hrair's 'Horizon' (2016). (Two channel video, HD.) Used by permission of the artist.

On the other hand, activists like Ibrahim and Dima still encourage mobilization, especially on social media—for instance, sustaining the #SaveGouta Campaign after attacks by government forces on civilians in February 2018. Ammar, Tarek, Jaber, and Tammam are also active, sharing posts related to the conflict or links for humanitarian donations, yet with less frequency. Despite this, a belief in the power of artistic creativity persists, to provide resilience to Syrians, but also to influence wider audiences' perspectives.

Syrians' condition resonates with Palestinians' because of their experience of prolonged displacement (Charles and Denman 2013). One may recall Palestinian poet Darwish's characterization of their status as sustained by an 'incurable malady called hope' (Boullata 2004, p. 82). Tammam phrased it clearly: 'Syrians are refugees now'. And how does their faith get configured in their own imagination, that of receiving countries, and of Syrian authorities? I raise the same open question as for future prospects for contemporary Syrian artists. As seen, their place has depended on specific imaginations of war and exile, encapsulated in the figure of a 'diaspora artist'. As more and more artists are based abroad and possibilities of working in Syria are almost null, it can be said that the Syrian art-scene has mobilized outside the country's borders. It is a crucial moment of uncertainty not only for artists, curators, and collectors, but also art-historians and academics, and I invite further reflection on what the future might bring.

As a final consideration, I would like to further reflect on my role of researcher. I have been encouraged by my informants, especially Ammar, to 'initiate a network of Syrian artists in London', 'transfer my knowledge into practice'. I am committed to the wider purpose of undoing the stereotypes that artists lament. As Van Willigen notes, larger numbers of anthropologists are working for government agencies and other organizations, with the objective of having an impact through policy-making (Van Willigen 2002, p. 3). As for the artistic realm, 'anthropologically informed visual practices' are increasingly used as 'social interventions' that unsettle mainstream representational practices by creating platforms for one's informants to represent their experiences (Pink 2009). In the near future, I am planning to collaborate with enterprises committed to promoting artists living in conflict zones such as today's Syria, in order to embrace Ammar's invitation to enable the application of academic research to artists' practical use.

Funding: This research received funding to cover part of the fieldwork from Green Templeton College, Oxford University.

Conflicts of Interest: The author declares no conflict of interest.

Appendix A

Interview and Topic Guide

I used this general interview and topic guide for all the interviews I carried out. This set of questions provided me with guidance throughout conversations with artists, but each took a different direction as I allowed much space for my informants to express themselves and for their perspectives to unfold. In fact, they frequently brought up new themes themselves, and I also prepared more specific questions concerning each artist's work.

Biography and Subjectivity

- I would like to know about your personal development as an artist and what brought you to focus on certain themes rather than others [specific artworks cited in this respect].
- Do you recreate specific moments of your past in your works? Do you tell a story about your own subjectivity?
- What are your artistic influences?
- When did you move here [London/France/Germany/Lebanon/Qatar]? How is your life as artist different compared to when you were in Syria?

Art and the Representation of Conflict

- I am interested in the relationship between art and the outside world. In your perspective, what is the role of art in society, and in particular in relation to the current crisis in Syria?
- How was your artistic production before the conflict? Has it changed since then, and if so, in what ways?
- What are your thoughts on the relationship between the production of art, resilience from conflict, and its representation? Can art foster resilience from conflict?
- As for the politics of representation around your works, how do you posit your art within the broader political and social framework of crisis and activism in Syria? I am referring in particular to the recently published book 'Syria Speaks', are you familiar with it?

- What would you like to communicate with your artworks? What are the main themes you deal with?
- Do you aim at giving a political commentary or simply representing reality, offering your distanced reflection on unfolding events?
- Have you encountered instances of external politicization? I mean, specific expectations by audiences or curators concerning the content of your work. Have you had to deal with 'wrong' interpretations that emphasize your political positioning in relation to what is happening in Syria? I would like to explore your take on this politicization lamented by other Syrian artists
- Do you agree that there is a particular social and political logic in being an artist coming from Syria at this particular point in time?

Doing Art in Syria versus Abroad

- Exhibitions often promote 'Syrian artists' as a group, and there is a general trend in the media to talk about 'Syrian art'. Do you feel part of this category?
- Do you feel like the tendency to group Syrian artists in a single category has brought many to isolate and take a different direction in their work?
- Can we talk of 'Syrian art'? Is there a style unique to Syrian artists that developed historically?
- What is your experience of the art-scene in Syria? How has it changed with the introduction of an art market?
- How is your life as an artist here like in comparison to Syria? How is your routine like? Where do you work? Are there good opportunities for artists?
- Do you engage in exchanges or work in collaboration with other Syrian artists here?
- Do you see your work related to that others treating similar themes? I can mention the names of the other artists I am interviewing for this research; do you know them or have you come across their work?
- Can we talk of a transnational network of Syrian artists, as the media does?
- What are the main artistic hubs for Syrian artists today?
- How do you see your future as a Syrian artist and that of your colleagues? How is it connected to Syria's future?
- What is your relation to Syria now? Do you have hope for your country?

References

Abbas, Hasan. 2005. Les artistes peintres syriens et la politique. *Collections Électroniques de l'Ifpo. Livres en Ligne des Presses de l'Institut Français du Proche-Orient* 22: 233–47.

Abbas, Hasan. 2014. Between the cultures of sectarianism and citizenship. In *Syria Speaks: Art and Culture from the Frontline*. Edited by Malu Halasa, Zaher Omareen and Nawara Mahfoud. London: Saqi.

Al-Khalidi, Ghazi. 1990. What the Arabs brought to Europe. (Oil on Canvas.). Available online: https://books.openedition.org/ifpo/564?lang=en (accessed on 10 January 2019).

Al-Shami, Leila. 2016. Emerging from the Kingdom of Silence. Beyond Institutions in Revolutionary Syria. Ibraaz. Available online: https://www.ibraaz.org/publications/75 (accessed on 4 January 2018).

Anderson, Brooke, and Don Duncan. 2010. Contemporary Middle East. Wall Street Journal. Available online: https://www.wsj.com/articles/SB127378397101791153 (accessed on 29 November 2017).

Anthias, Floya. 1998. Evaluating 'diaspora': Beyond ethnicity? *Sociology* 32: 557–80.

Appadurai, Arjun. 1988. Putting hierarchy in its place. *Cultural Anthropology* 3: 36–49. [CrossRef]

Araeen, Rasheed, Sean Cubitt, and Ziauddin Sardar, eds. 2002. *The Third Text Reader: On Art, Culture, and Theory*. London: Bloomsbury Publishing.

Becker, Carmen. 2005. Strategies of Power Consolidation in Syria under Bashar al-Asad: Modernizing Control over Resources. *The Arab Studies Journal* 13: 65–91.

Belting, Hans, and Andrea Buddensieg. 2009. *The Global Art World. Audiences, Markets, and Museums*. Ostfildern: Hatje Cantz.

Bernard, H. Russell. 2017. *Research Methods in Anthropology: Qualitative and Quantitative Approaches*. Lanham: Rowman & Littlefield.

Bevan, Sara. 2015. *Art from Contemporary Conflict*. London: Imperial War Museum.

Boëx, Cécile. 2011. The end of the state monopoly over culture: Toward the commodification of cultural and artistic production. *Middle East Critique* 20: 139–55. [CrossRef]

Boëx, Cécile. 2013. Mobilisations d'artistes dans le mouvement de révolte en Syrie: Modes d'action et limites de l'engagement. In *Devenir Révolutionnaires. Au Cœur des Révoltes Arabes*. Paris: Armand Colin, pp. 87–112.

Boullata, Kamal. 2004. Art under the Siege. *Journal of Palestine Studies* 33: 70–84. [CrossRef]

Bourke, Joanna. 2017. *War and Art*. London: Reaktion Books.

Brownell, Ginanne. 2014. Syrian Artists Set up Base in Beirut. The New York Times. Available online: https://www.nytimes.com/2014/06/19/arts/international/syrian-artists-set-up-base-in-beirut.html (accessed on 21 January 2018).

Buchakjian, Gregory. 2012. *War and Other Impossible Possibilities: Thoughts on Arab History and Contemporary Art*. Beirut: Alarm Editions.

Candea, Matei. 2007. Arbitrary locations: In defence of the bounded field-site. *Journal of the Royal Anthropological Institute* 13: 167–84. [CrossRef]

Carver, Antonia. 2006. Don't Force Middle Eastern Artists into an Identity Straitjacket. The Guardian. Available online: https://www.theguardian.com/commentisfree/2006/sep/06/arts.visualarts (accessed on 20 January 2018).

Chakrabarty, D. 2000. Subaltern studies and postcolonial historiography. *Nepantla: Views from South* 1: 9–32.

Chakrabarty, Dipesh. 2009. *Provincializing Europe: Postcolonial Thought and Historical Difference*. Princeton: Princeton University Press.

Charles, Lorraine, and Kate Denman. 2013. Syrian and Palestinian Syrian refugees in Lebanon: The plight of women and children. *Journal of International Women's Studies* 14: 96.

Chaudhary, Ali R., and Dana M. Moss. 2016. *Triadic Political Opportunity Structures: Re-conceptualising Immigrant Transnational Politics*. Working Paper 129. Oxford: International Migration Institute (IMI).

Clifford, James. 1997. Diasporas. In *Routes: Travel and Translation in the late Twentieth Century*. Cambridge: Harvard University Press, pp. 244–77.

Cohen, Robin. 2008. *Global Diasporas: An Introduction*, 2nd ed. London: Routledge.

Cooke, Miriam. 2007. *Dissident Syria: Making Oppositional Arts Official*. Durham: Duke University Press.

Cooke, Miriam. 2016. *Dancing in Damascus: Creativity, Resilience, and the Syrian Revolution*. Abingdon: Taylor & Francis.

De Cesari, Chiara. 2012. Anticipatory Representation: Building the Palestinian Nation (-State) through Artistic Performance. *Studies in Ethnicity and Nationalism* 12: 82–100. [CrossRef]

Deebi, Aissa. 2012. Who I Am, Where I Come from, and Where I Am Going: A Critical Study of Arab Diaspora as Creative Space. Ph.D. dissertation, University of Southampton, Southampton, UK.

DP News. 2010. Contemporary Middle East. DP News. Available online: http://www.dp-news.com/en/detail.aspx?articleid=38991 (accessed on 6 December 2017).

Duclos, Diane. 2017. When ethnography does not rhyme with anonymity: Reflections on name disclosure, self-censorship and storytelling. *Ethnography*. [CrossRef]

Duncan, Don. 2010. Contemporary art from Syria Finds Favour with International Buyers. DW. Available online: http://www.dw.com/en/contemporary-art-from-syria-finds-favor-with-international-buyers/a-5493328 (accessed on 15 November 2017).

Elkins, James, ed. 2007. *Is Art History Global?* Abingdon: Taylor & Francis, vol. 3.

Elkins, James, Zhivka Valiavicharska, and Alice Kim. 2010. *Art and Globalization*. University Park: Penn State Press, vol. 1.

Farjam, Lisa. 2009. *Unveiled: New Art from the Middle East*. London: Booth-Clibborn Editions.

Foley, Sean. 2013. When life imitates art: The Arab Spring, the Middle East, and the modern world. *Alternatives: Turkish Journal of International Relations* 12: 32–46.

Gardner, Anthony, and Green Green. 2013. Biennials of the South on the Edges of the Global. *Third Text* 27: 442–55. [CrossRef]

Gellner, David N. 2012. Uncomfortable antinomies: Going beyond methodological nationalism in social and cultural anthropology. In *Beyond Methodological Nationalism*. London: Routledge, pp. 127–44.

Given, Lisa M., ed. 2008. *The Sage Encyclopedia of Qualitative Research Methods*. Thousand Oaks: Sage Publications.

Glick-Schiller, Nina, Linda Basch, and Cristina Blanc-Szanton, eds. 1992. Transnationalism: A new analytic framework for understanding migration. In *Towards a Transnational Perspective on Migration*. New York: The New York Academy of Sciences, vol. 645, pp. 1–24.

Griswold, Eliza. 2018. Mapping the Journeys of Syria's artists. The New Yorker. Available online: https://www.newyorker.com/culture/culture-desk/mapping-the-journeys-of-syrias-artists (accessed on 28 January 2018).

Groys, Boris. 2008. *Art Power*. Cambridge: MIT Press.

Guillemin, Marilys, and Lynn Gillam. 2004. Ethics, reflexivity, and "ethically important moments" in research. *Qualitative Inquiry* 10: 261–80. [CrossRef]

Gupta, Akhil, and James Ferguson. 1997. Culture, power, place: Ethnography at the end of an era. In *Culture, Power, Place. Explorations in Critical Anthropology*. Durham: Duke University Press.

Halasa, Malu. 2012. Creative Dissent. *Index on Censorship* 41: 14–25. [CrossRef]

Harris, Clare E. 2006. The Buddha Goes Global: Some thoughts towards a transnational art history. *Art History* 29: 698–720. [CrossRef]

Harris, Clare E. 2012a. *The Museum on the Roof of the World: Art, Politics, and the Representation of Tibet*. Chicago: University of Chicago Press.

Harris, Clare E. 2012b. In and out of Place: Tibetan Artists' Travels in the Contemporary Art World. *Visual Anthropology Review* 28: 152–63. [CrossRef]

Heydemann, Steven. 2013. Syria and the Future of Authoritarianism. *Journal of Democracy* 24: 59–73. [CrossRef]

Hokayem, Emile. 2013. *Syria's Uprising and the Fracturing of the Levant*. London: Routledge.

Holmes, Seth M., and Heide Castañeda. 2016. Representing the "European refugee crisis" in Germany and beyond: Deservingness and difference, life and death. *American Ethnologist* 43: 12–24. [CrossRef]

Homsey, Dakota D. 2016. The Art of Exile: A Narrative for Social Justice in a Modern World. *Student Publications*. 421. Available online: http://cupola.gettysburg.edu/student_scholarship/421 (accessed on 15 November 2017).

Jelinek, Alana. 2013. *This Is Not Art: Activism and Other 'Not-Art'*. London: IB Tauris.

Karp, Ivan, and Steven D. Lavine. 1991. *Exhibiting Cultures*. Washington, DC: Smithsonian Institute Press.

Kaur, Raminder, and Parul Dave-Mukherji. 2014. *Arts and Aesthetics in a Globalising World*. London: Bloomsbury Publishing.

Kluijver, Robert. 2009. Syrian Artists Cherish Their Cultural Background. The Power of Culture. Available online: http://kvc.minbuza.nl/en/current/2009/august/syrian-artists (accessed on 26 December 2017).

Krauss, Rosalind E. 1986. *The Originality of the Avant-Garde and Other Modernist Myths*. Cambridge: MIT Press.

Kräussl, Roman. 2014. Art as an Alternative Asset Class: Risk and Return Characteristics of the Middle Eastern & Northern African Art Markets. *SSRN Electronic Journal*. [CrossRef]

Langton, Marcia, and Nikos Papastergiadis. 2003. *Complex Entanglements: Art, Globalisation, and Cultural Difference*. London, Sydney, and Chicago: Rivers Oram Press.

Lenssen, Anneka Erin. 2014. The Shape of the Support: Painting and Politics in Syria's Twentieth Century. Ph.D. dissertation, Massachusetts Institute of Technology, Cambridge, MA, USA.

Little, Tom. 2011. Syrian Protesters Set Up Celebrity List of Shame. BBC Monitoring. Available online: http://www.bbc.co.uk/news/world-middle-east-16284426 (accessed on 2 February 2018).

Longuenesse, Elisabeth, and Cyril Roussel. 2014. *Retour sur Une Expérience Historique: La Crise Syrienne en Perspective*. Beirut: Presses de l'Ifpo, Cahiers de l'Ifpo, p. 8. ISBN 978-2-35159-402-5. Available online: https://books.openedition.org/ifpo/6526 (accessed on 10 January 2019).

Mackinlay, John. 2003. Artists and war. *The RUSI Journal* 148: 20–23. [CrossRef]

Malmvig, Helle. 2016. Eyes Wide Shut: Power and Creative Visual Counter-Conducts in the Battle for Syria, 2011–2014. *Global Society* 30: 258–78. [CrossRef]

Marcus, George E. 1995. Ethnography in/of the world system: The emergence of multi-sited ethnography. *Annual Review of Anthropology* 24: 95–117. [CrossRef]

Marcus, George E., and Fred R. Myers, eds. 1995. *The Traffic in Culture: Refiguring Art and Anthropology*. Berkeley: University of California Press.

Naficy, Hamid. 1991. The poetics and practice of Iranian nostalgia in exile. *Diaspora: A Journal of Transnational Studies* 1: 285–302. [CrossRef]

Oweis, Khaled Yacoub. 2010. Feature—Damascus Art Gallery Ignites Syrian Culture War in Reuters. Available online: https://www.reuters.com/article/syria-art-idAFLDE6961JG20101013 (accessed on 30 January 2018).

Pearlman, Wendy. 2017. *We Crossed a Bridge and it Trembled: Voices from Syria*. New York: HarperCollins.

Pink, Sarah, ed. 2009. *Visual Interventions: Applied Visual Anthropology*. New York: Berghahn Books, vol. 4.

Porter, Venetia. 2006. *Word into Art: Artists of the Modern Middle East*. London: British Museum Press.

Qayyum, Mehrunisa. 2011. *Syrian Diaspora: Cultivating a New Public Space Consciousness*. Policy Brief. No 35. Washington, DC: Middle East Institute.

Roudi-Fahimi, Farzaneh, and Mary Mederios Kent. 2007. Challenges and opportunities: The population of the Middle East and North Africa. *Population Bulletin* 62: 24.

Safran, William. 1991. Diasporas in modern societies: Myths of homeland and return. *Diaspora: A Journal of Transnational Studies* 1: 83–99. [CrossRef]

Salih, Ruba, and Sophie Richter-Devroe. 2014. Cultures of resistance in Palestine and beyond: On the politics of art, aesthetics, and affect. *The Arab Studies Journal* 22: 8–27.

Schneider, Arnd. 1996. Uneasy relationships: Contemporary artists and anthropology. *Journal of Material Culture* 1: 183–210. [CrossRef]

Schneider, Arnd, ed. 2017. *Alternative Art and Anthropology: Global Encounters*. London: Bloomsbury Publishing.

Schultheis, Franz, Erwin Single, Raphaela Köfeler, and Thomas Mazzurana. 2016. *Art Unlimited?: Dynamics and Paradoxes of a Globalizing Art World*. Bielefeld: Transcript-Verlag.

Seaman, Anna. 2016. Christie's and Sotheby's Make a Bid to Boost Middle East Art. The National. Available online: https://www.thenational.ae/arts-culture/christie-s-and-sotheby-s-make-a-bid-to-boost-middle-east-art-1.167781 (accessed on 5 March 2018).

Shabout, Nada. 2012. In between, Fragmented and Disoriented Art Making in Iraq. *Middle East Report* 263: 38–43.

Shannon, Jonathan H. 2005. Metonyms of modernity in contemporary Syrian music and painting. *Ethnos* 70: 361–86. [CrossRef]

Sottimano, Aurora. 2016. Building authoritarian 'legitimacy': Domestic compliance and international standing of Bashar al-Asad's Syria. *Global Discourse* 6: 450–66. [CrossRef]

Stone Fish, Isaac. 2013. The Massive Mural That Captures Syria's Surprising Alliance with North Korea. Foreign Policy. Available online: http://foreignpolicy.com/2013/09/10/the-massive-mural-that-captures-syrias-surprising-alliance-with-north-korea/ (accessed on 26 January 2018).

Takieddine, Zena. 2011. Arab Art in a Changing World. *Contemporary Practices* 8: 54–61.

Taylor, Charles. 1994. *Multiculturalism*. Princeton: Princeton University Press.

Toukan, Hanan. 2013. Negotiating Representation, Re-making War: Transnationalism, Counter-hegemony and Contemporary Art ftom Post-Taif Beirut. In *Narrating Conflict in the Middle East: Discourse, Image and Communications Practices in Lebanon and Palestine*. Edited by Dina Matar and Zahera Harb. London: IB Tauris, vol. 121.

UN News. 2018. Syria. Available online: https://news.un.org/en/focus/syria (accessed on 22 April 2018).

Van Willigen, John. 2002. *Applied Anthropology: An Introduction*. Westport: Greenwood Publishing Group.

Vignal, Leïla. 2012. *Syria: Anatomy of a Revolution*. Paris: Books and Ideas.

Wade, Mike. 2017. SNP Denies Trying to Shape Artists' Ideas. The Sunday Times. Available online: https://www.thetimes.co.uk/article/snp-denies-trying-to-shape-artists-ideas-l6bctfqsc (accessed on 3 March 2018).

Walker-Parker, Sharon LaVon. 2005. Embodied Exile: Contemporary Iranian Women Artists and the Politics of Place. Ph.D. thesis, University of Arizona, Tucson, AZ, USA.

Weeden, Lisa. 2015. *Ambiguities of Domination*. Chicago: University of Chicago Press.

Welsch, Robert L. 2004. Epilogue: The authenticity of constructed art worlds. *Visual Anthropology* 17: 401–6. [CrossRef]

Wimmer, Andreas, and Nina Glick-Schiller. 2002. Methodological nationalism and the study of migration. *European Journal of Sociology* 43: 217–40. [CrossRef]

Winegar, Jessica. 2008a. *Creative Reckonings*. Cairo: The American University in Cairo Press.
Winegar, Jessica. 2008b. The humanity game: Art, Islam, and the war on terror. *Anthropological Quarterly* 81: 651–68. [CrossRef]
Withey, Andrew John. 2013. Contemporary, Emigrant, Middle Eastern Art. Ph.D. dissertation, University of Sussex, Brighton, UK.
Wolcott, Harry F. 2005. *The Art of Fieldwork*. Lanham: Rowman Altamira.
Woodcock, L. 2012. The Development and Differentiation of the Market for Contemporary Syrian Art: 2006–2012. Master's thesis, Sotheby's Institute of Art, Claremont, CA, USA.
Young, James O. 2010. *Cultural Appropriation and the Arts*. Hoboken: John Wiley & Sons.
Ziff, Bruce, and Pratima V. Rao, eds. 1997. *Borrowed Power: Essays on Cultural Appropriation*. New Brunswick: Rutgers University Press.
Zinn, Howard. 2011. *Artists in Times of War*. New York: Seven Stories Press.

© 2019 by the author. Licensee MDPI, Basel, Switzerland. This article is an open access article distributed under the terms and conditions of the Creative Commons Attribution (CC BY) license (http://creativecommons.org/licenses/by/4.0/).

MDPI
St. Alban-Anlage 66
4052 Basel
Switzerland
Tel. +41 61 683 77 34
Fax +41 61 302 89 18
www.mdpi.com

Arts Editorial Office
E-mail: arts@mdpi.com
www.mdpi.com/journal/arts

www.ingramcontent.com/pod-product-compliance
Lightning Source LLC
LaVergne TN
LVHW072000080526
838202LV00064B/6800